Praise for The Competency Curriculum Toolkit

We know that young people learn best when the curriculum they meet is coherent, when it makes sense to them because of a real purpose, in a proper context. It is the bringing together of subject knowledge and understanding with skills and with personal qualities and attributes that creates progress.

Making progress means developing competencies and, if young people are aware of how their competence develops, they can learn and recognise their growth.

The Competency Curriculum Toolkit builds personal, learning and thinking skills through carefully constructed activity and well designed pathways.

It is a superb toolkit. It has the right instrument for the right job and the teacher's task is to work out what the youngsters need. It oozes with practical suggestions, practical ideas and opportunites for young people.

Enjoy it… and use it.

Professor Mick Waters

The book starts with a dramatic reminder of what skills a school leaver will need in the twenty-first Century - and the point is already made. Mostly we teach 'stuff' - when what we desperately need to teach are the competencies to cope with a fast changing, knowledge-based future. Self-management skills and the creative/analytical skills needed to take advantage of the abundance of information that are now just a few key strokes away on everyone's computer.

The book's triumph is to show how any school can 'smuggle' those skills into the curriculum via exciting cross curricular projects that students will see are directly relevant to their current and future lives. This book should be the guide for every Year 7 teacher - and would go a very long way to launching a new breed of can-do self sufficient learners.

Colin Rose, Founder Accelerated Learning Systems

This is a rich, exemplary handbook for the kind of competency-focussed KS3 curriculum that we have been moving towards for several years and is now fully promoted by QCA. It answers all the questions that hold many managers and teachers back: why should we change; what will the benefits be; how do we genuinely integrate PLTS and subject-specific content; how do we plan themed projects; how do we timetable them; how do we ensure rigour; how do we assess?

The Competency Curriculum Toolkit informs, excites, guides and resources. Better still, Jackie and Helen invite you to customise and create; they provide lots of detailed, workable ideas that will accelerate your planning, but each project has enough room for you to embellish the frameworks and activities. Best of all, the book provides you with models and examples — patterns that show you how to devise your own unique themed projects. It gets you into a modern, holistic way of thinking about curriculum design and classroom delivery.

The timing of the book could not be better. In many ways, the conceptual battle has been won — most people accept the urgent need for generic skills and attitudes to be deliberately taught alongside traditional curriculum content. However, this emerging national priority is leaving teachers hungry for practical applications. 'The Competency Curriculum', with its wisdom and pragmatism, satisfies the professional appetite. It fills the gap between embracing and implementing some big, important ideas.

Paul Ginnis, author *The Teachers Toolkit*

In the twenty first century illiteracy is not just about being unable to read and write, it is about the inability to learn how to learn. The Toolkit will help convince the doubters that a 'Key Competencies' approach is vital. After reading through it, I am convinced more than ever that the development of PLTS is not a way to motivate, develop, engage, challenge and inspire young people, it is THE way. The review of theory is comprehensive, the resources are excellent, the projects engaging and the tracking tool simple and effective. For those who are hesitating it is a great 'way in' and for those who are well down the road it will enhance what they are already doing. The art of teaching meets the science of learning!

John Jones writer, presenter and educational consultant

According to Einstein, you can't solve the problems by using the same thinking that caused them. If we school children the way we were schooled then we are in serious trouble when it comes to the challenges of the 21st century. In your hands, with this wonderful new book, is a tool that can transform the nature of education in this country and beyond. And don't let the 'death of subject knowledge' naysayers distract you. Jackie and Helen are not talking about doing away with knowledge. They are describing in detail, in easy steps, in a systematic and proven manner, how you can help children acquire knowledge in a way that teaches them the skills to survive whatever the twenty first century throws at them, and do better at school in the process. This powerful and practical book from genuine educational pioneers has made it easy for you. Your challenge is to decide whether you are brave enough to do what this book asks of you. For everyone's sake let's hope you are.

Ian Gilbert, Founder Independent Thinking Ltd

The Competency Curriculum Toolkit

Developing PLTS Through Themed Learning

- Engaging learners through collaborative approaches
- Opening minds for independent thinking
- Tracking progress in the PLTS

Jackie Beere and Helen Boyle

The Competency Curriculum Toolkit

Developing PLTS Through Themed Learning

Jackie Beere and Helen Boyle

Crown House Publishing Ltd
www.crownhouse.co.uk
www.crownhousepublishing.com

First published by
Crown House Publishing Ltd
Crown Buildings, Bancyfelin, Carmarthen, Wales, SA33 5ND, UK
www.crownhouse.co.uk

and

Crown House Publishing Company LLC
6 Trowbridge Drive, Suite 5, Bethel, CT 06801, USA
www.crownhousepublishing.com

British Library of Cataloguing-in-Publication Data
A catalogue entry for this book is available
from the British Library.

13-digit ISBN 978-184590126-4

LCCN 2008936797

Printed and bound in the UK by
Cromwell Press Group

Acknowledgements

We would like to thank the students of Campion School who were part of the Opening Minds curriculum pilot courses in 2004 and 2005. They enjoyed the 'joined up learning' so much that they convinced us this was the right way to engage Key Stage 3 in learning. They taught us that learning at KS3 could be exciting, challenging and truly cross-curricular, as well as developing personal skills in emotional intelligence. Thank you 'Team Awesome'!

We would like to acknowledge the inspiration of Mick Waters, who has implemented his vision of real learning through his role at QCA and also Professor David Hargreaves, whose drive to develop truly personalised learning has transformed secondary education. It has been our privilege to work with many other visionary colleagues for many years. We would like to thank all those talented and courageous teachers, who are engaged in transforming learning in their schools on a day-to-day basis. We know they will take this toolkit and use it, adapt it and develop it to make amazing lessons for lucky kids.

None of this would be possible without the work of the RSA, in particular Lesley James, leading a brave, new approach to secondary education.

Working with a publisher like Crown House has been a great pleasure and we would like to thank David, Bev, Tom, Les, Nobbie and all the team for their continuous support.

Jackie and Helen

And in addition …

Special thanks to my daughter Lucy and all her KS3 students at Unity College who have tried out so many of these materials. I would like to thank my husband John for working so hard on the curriculum links, the proofreading, the index and the constant encouragement. Finally, I would like to pay tribute to my youngest daughter Carrie, who has had the hardest year but keeps proving that all this emotional intelligence stuff really works.

Jackie Beere

I would like to thank my family; especially my parents who continue to give me endless supplies of love and support in countless ways.

Thank you to my two darling boys, Euan and Oscar, you make me smile and watch in wonder at your relentless curiosity of the world around you.

Finally I would like to thank my wonderful husband Gavin for his never-ending patience, encouragement and support—thank goodness, our lives are never dull!

Helen Boyle

Contents

Section 4

Foreword

The world, not just the world of education, has changed forever and it's vital that we're open to knowledge and new thinking, whatever the source. Abu Yasuf Al-Kindi (805–873), the Islamic philosopher and scholar, put it very eloquently:

> *We should not shy away from welcoming and acquiring the truth regardless of where it comes from, even if it comes from distant races and nations that are different from us. Nothing is more important than seeking the truth except the truth itself.*

Due to modern means of communication, technology and transportation the world is suddenly very small. An idea that originates in one part of the world can be almost simultaneously shared with others on the other side of the globe. You might think that the world has enough information and data. But it wants more—and it wants it faster. It wants to look for the links and connections.

In the past knowledge was like gold: it gave you power, influence and wealth. Now knowledge is like milk: if you keep it too long, it becomes out of date and stagnant.

There is a constant evolution of thinking and ideas that more and more people are tapping into and sharing. Competitors are becoming collaborators. People that previously would hold on to what they had and knew have come to the realisation that it is through the sharing of their knowledge and experience that they keep their thinking sharp and their actions, businesses and institutions effective. In short, their survival is now dependent on the distribution, not hoarding, of knowledge. Governments are also realising this. This truth was reinforced for me over the past week with staggering clarity.

I write this on a plane following a two-day conference on education held in Abu Dhabi. The audience demographic was amazingly disparate. From western academics in 'our-man-in-Havana' style suits with sensible brogues to groups of Arabic female primary teachers (all primary teachers in Abu Dhabi are women) dressed in the traditional black burkah, revealing nothing but their eyes. For two days they attended keynote lectures—from the neurology of learning to the changing face of Arabic education in the twenty-first century—delivered by educators from the West and the East.

The audience were exposed to challenging ideas and activities. They were given research, data and practical examples to prove that subject-specific education is less effective for the majority of students and that it is not only possible, but desirable, for teachers to stop working so hard at their planning and focus more on letting children own their own learning.

Among these programmes and workshops was one that stood out in its relevance and capacity to link all of these ideas in one clear and amazingly effective process. It was the competency-led curriculum delivered with energy, humour and intelligence by Jackie Beere, who was sharing the contents of her recent contribution to the world of educational thinking, which happens to be the book you are holding now.

In this book Jackie and her co-author Helen Boyle have provided a timely solution to the challenges facing educators; not just in the UK, but globally. The response to the ideas and process from those that were fortunate enough to have attended Jackie's workshops was nothing short of remarkable. I am not sure she managed to have any time to herself having to deal with the numbers of people that stayed behind requesting further conversations and to discuss ideas.

The majority of educators attending the conference in Abu Dhabi had travelled from all over the UAE (United Arab Emirates). They arrived with questions and a thirst for ideas. Not, I have to say, with a desire to take everything wholesale but to make sure it built off their own ideas, experiences and history.

Fortunately the universal truths that were exposed by the speakers were very well received. Delegates were open-minded and posed critical and challenging questions. In observing the response of the delegates to these ideas I realised that Helen and Jackie's book has appeared at just the right time.

It is rare that a publication arrives to provide insights, examples and immediate solutions to challenges and questions for thousands (if not millions) of people at the exactly the right moment in history. It is no exaggeration to say that this is one of those books.

I know that many of the delegates will now be applying principles and ideas shared by Jackie. I know this because I am one of them. Next week I am working not only with schools but with a global business and intend to share them with others. As a fellow speaker it is a rare joy to come from a conference with more insight than you took to it. Jackie and Helen have enabled me to do just that.

My primary reason for writing the foreword was to note a word of warning to schools, particularly those in the UK. We, in the UK, have a long and rich history of taking our ideas, inventions and values around the world and sharing them with other nations. Over the past fifty years we have seen a growing number of skilled individuals and their ideas leaving our shores and being applied by other countries more readily. I believe this is because we ponder too long and change too slowly. We are comfortable and find change disturbing. But others don't.

The United Arab Emirates has grown massively over the past forty years and does not want to stop. They see the answer to their sustained growth in educating and developing the life skills of young people who can contribute effectively in a global village. They know that the world is changing and are looking to the future and building off the past.

Jackie, Helen and others like them are sharing their knowledge, not keeping it to themselves. The movement for global cooperation in education is vital if we are going to help shape citizens of the world who have the competencies for thinking, learning, listening, changing, imagining and solving problems.

My big concern is that we in the UK will still be dawdling at the edges of innovation (innovation that was generated in the UK) while the rest of the world gets on and puts that knowledge into action.

Finally, I would encourage you not to just buy this book, but to regularly take if off the shelf and use it. *Use it to create the curriculum that will transform learning in your school.* To quote from the Buddha, another global influencer:

If you know, but do not do, you do not know.

Roy Leighton

Introduction

This book has been written in response to many requests from teachers and curriculum leaders for something 'to help us on the way to creating our competency-based curriculum'. It is not a programme, a manual or a 'how to do' book. It is a resource in four sections. Section 1 is a review of the theory that led us to consider re-designing our UK curriculum. Section 2 is packed full of resources: work schemes for some exemplar projects and associated lessons which show how they may be delivered. Section 3 contains some more loosely structured 'breakthrough' projects for Year 8 or alternative blocked day approaches. There is an electronic Tracker Pack to accompany Section 4 that offers some ideas on how both the student and the teacher can track progress in the competences as they develop. The case studies given throughout the book demonstrate how powerful this learning can be in real schools. You will find some of this toolkit useful for training and some useful for delivering your new curriculum but, above all, it is meant to be adapted to become bespoke for your own school and context.

We have a fantastic opportunity to change the experience of students in Key Stage 3, so that instead of plateauing through KS3, they take off as engaged learners into KS4. It is our experience that this more active, collaborative curriculum delivers a new range of skills which encourage learners to become independent and self-managing. We had two overriding priorities for the competency curriculum approach proposed in this book:

■ That it must nurture an independent and emotionally intelligent young person who takes more responsibility for his or her own learning.

■ That it must be rigorous, challenging and able to demonstrate progress in the personal, learning and thinking skills (PLTS) and in subject-specific skills.

It has been written to try to provide inspiration, motivation, examples and ideas to help teachers find a path through the difficult task of planning, writing and resourcing a competency curriculum. In writing this book, we have realised what a complex process it is to develop your own new curriculum, evaluate it and evolve it to suit your students. This book aims to give you ideas that will help you take the first steps in a process that will take several years; building a competency curriculum is not a quick fix, but the start of a long, exciting journey.

How to use this toolkit

Prepare

The first two chapters provide essential background information about the context of the major changes in the curriculum brought about by the Qualifications and Curriculum Authority (QCA) in 2008. These chapters put the needs of learners in a global context and there are PowerPoint presentations on the CD-ROM to help you deliver the messages about twenty-first century learning to the staff at your school.

Decisions

The personal, learning and thinking skills are the competences we have chosen to use in this toolkit.

The PLTS

Team workers

Self-managers

Independent enquirers

Effective participators

Reflective learners

Creative thinkers

The PLTS have evolved from the early work on the Opening Minds curriculum by the Royal Society of Arts (RSA). They are now recommended by QCA and will be integrated into the Diplomas at KS4. It makes sense to use these as competences because they seem to contain all the skills a student will need for learning in the twenty-first century. However, you may wish to add literacy or other competences of your own choosing. Alternatively, you could group the competences together for easier assessment as we have done later in the Tracker Pack (Section 4). The English Speaking and Listening Assessment of Pupil Progress (APP) progression model could also be used to help assessment in the classroom and as a powerful addition to your tracking audit. The

students spend most of their time communicating with each other in this type of curriculum so it makes sense for them to measure their progress in this essential skill.

Chapter 3 outlines the options for delivering a competency curriculum. There are many possible methods of delivery. However, we have provided resources for our favourite model, which is for a KS3 programme that delivers a high percentage of competency teaching in Year 7. This then moves to a student-designed project model in Year 8, alongside more subject specialism and then into further subject specialism in Year 9.

In addition, it is recommended that the ultimate outcome of the two to three year programme is an accredited, independent 'project' at Level 1 or 2 (AQA or Edexcel). In this the students will create their own learning assignment which will be their first experience of exam success. Through this model the purpose of KS3 will be to help nurture independent learners who have great learning 'habits' and an excellent understanding of what the PLTS are and how to develop them in their KS4 courses.

Competency projects: Setting PLTS lesson objectives and delivering essential subject skills		
Year 7 – Up to 50% of curriculum will be competence/ project based led.	Year 8 – up to 30% of curriculum will be competence/ project based led with a greater emphasis placed on students to design their own projects.	Year 9 – up to 10% of curriculum to be competence/ project based led, leading to a project delivering 0.5 GCSE.

Implement

The toolkit in Section 2 offers sample schemes of work, ready-to-use lesson plans and teacher's notes for four projects which aim to deliver half a term's work each (depending upon how much timetable time you give to the projects). These projects provide examples which can be used off-the-shelf but it is recommended that they are adapted to your context and your students.

In particular there are the following recommendations:

Localise

Create an additional project that fits your locality and engages students with their community. You can do this using the blank pro-forma found on the CD-ROM.

Learn to learn first

Brain Breakthrough (Project 1) contains many lessons from *The Learner's Toolkit* by Jackie Beere (2007). It is included here as the first project because it is important to train students early in the basic neuroscience they need in o   ) believe that they can be great learners. It will also introduce them to the notion of learning styles and preferences in order for them to take more responsibility for their own learning. An important aspect of this is for the students to realise that their brain will grow and change as they learn. Learning to Learn is about flexibility, responsibility and reflection, which are all useful skills to apply to the rest of this programme of study. This part of the course and indeed the whole competency approach will also deliver and develop the Social and Emotional Aspects of Learning (SEAL).

Subjects to be included

You will need to decide which subjects you want to include in your competency curriculum. You will notice that curriculum links are included for all the projects outlined in this book. It is advised that similar links are included in order to reassure staff that subject-specific skills and content are delivered in the projects studied, as well as the PLTS competences. The team planning the projects should involve the appropriate specialist teachers from the subjects included.

Progression – more co-designed projects

In Section 3 we introduce Breakthrough Projects. These are exciting, loosely structured projects that allow more freedom of choice in the activities for students. It is our experience that students really engage with this type of learning and that it can deliver the PLTS effectively. These projects can be used to progress towards even more student centred activities. They can also be used as one-off PLTS days or PSHE/Citizenship lessons. They include suggested activities based on the multiple intelligence model but also have the option for students to create their own activities. It is recommended that students work out success criteria for all of the tasks which they design in order to ensure high quality outcomes. The assessment of the PLTS during these activities by students and teachers will help students develop a more independent approach to prepare them for planning their own project for accreditation later.

Praise and advice

Assessment for learning techniques involves self- and peer-assessment and this is an essential aspect of the learning that takes place in a competency curriculum. The praise and advice model seen in some of the projects is a simple device to help students support each others' learning on a regular basis throughout their project and at the end of it.

Assessment – towards 'golden learning'

The Tracker Pack and CD-ROM assessment tool is a suggested means to help assess competency-based learning. It is suggested that a paper copy of the Tracker Pack is kept by students for regular assessment sessions. The electronic version can then be used to summarise this paper copy and can be supplemented by the teacher's grading which can be reported to parents. However, its main purpose is to track progress against specific criteria and share with students how progress is being made in the competences and how targets should be set. The notion of 'golden learning' is a method we have used that has been popular but many schools use the terms *developing, progressing, mastery* or other preferred descriptors of levels. As mentioned earlier, the APP progression models can be used if additional tracking in core or foundation subjects is required.

Please note: Recording National Curriculum (NC) levels for subjects other than core may not be practical or possible when implementing a competency approach, so qualitative reporting and self-assessment is recommended. In addition, QCA will be bringing out a progression model for the PLTS in 2009. This may eventually be the chosen tool for assessing progress into the future.

> **TOP TIP** The ideal experience for students would be to have the same teacher, in the same classroom, with easy access to laptops.
>
> This aspiration for implementation of the work described in this book could determine the success or failure of your new curriculum.

The twenty-first century learning school

This diagram shows how the elements of SEAL provide the roots of emotional intelligence that could be at the heart of the school vision. The trunk of the tree represents the curriculum that can deliver the Personal, Learning and Thinking skills (PLTS) across the whole curriculum. The leaves and blossom are the aims of the curriculum which is reflected in the delivery of the Every Child Matters outcomes for young people.

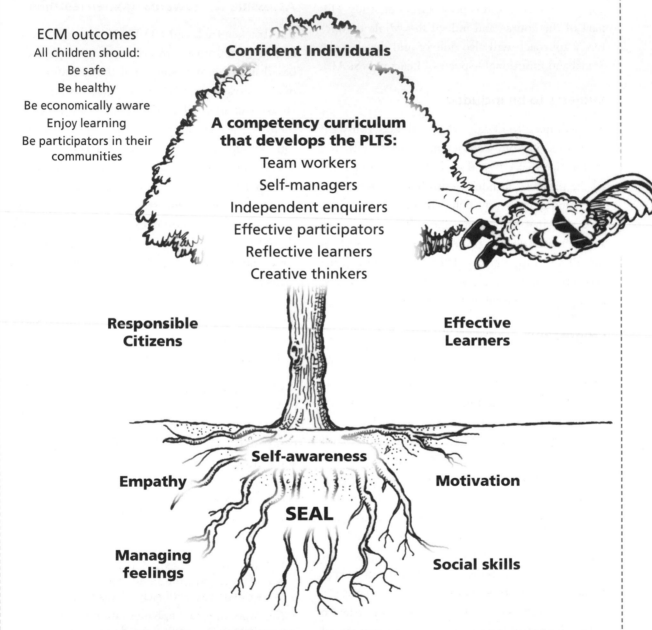

ECM outcomes
All children should:
Be safe
Be healthy
Be economically aware
Enjoy learning
Be participators in their communities

Confident Individuals

A competency curriculum that develops the PLTS:
Team workers
Self-managers
Independent enquirers
Effective participators
Reflective learners
Creative thinkers

Responsible Citizens

Effective Learners

Self-awareness

Empathy

Motivation

SEAL

Managing feelings

Social skills

We would like to wish you the very best of luck implementing your new curriculum and using these resources. No doubt by the time this book is published there will be further evidence to support the need for a competency curriculum in secondary schools that will develop learners who will love learning and thrive in the global economy.

If you have any doubts about whether or not to make this happen, consider this question: What do you remember learning during your secondary school education in KS3?

Jackie Beere
Helen Boyle

Section 1

Chapter 1
Essential Learning for the Twenty-first Century

Why we need a competency-based curriculum

WANTED

FOR THE TWENTY-FIRST CENTURY GLOBAL WORKFORCE:

Resilient, creative independent learners who have flexible skills and competences, who work well in teams and can lead themselves and others to perform up to and beyond their potential.

Do we produce the above now in our schools? If not, how can we?

Key questions:

- Should the curriculum be organised around subjects or skills?

- How can we teach students emotional intelligence and self-management skills?

- Who should be teaching them—teachers, other adults, other students, online tutors?

- How can we ensure that students transfer their skills and knowledge from one subject area to another encouraging independent, flexible learning capacity?

- How can we ensure that we are developing creative thinkers and risk takers?

- How can we make sure that even disruptive students 'choose to learn'?

There is a growing global desire to find out just what we need to change in our education systems that will make the difference; the difference between producing pupils who simply pass (or fail) exams and producing independent lifelong learners who can thrive in the new fast moving, knowledge-based economy.

Our contention is that we need to fundamentally change our methods of learning and teaching, especially for KS3. There are many theories of learning, such as Howard Gardner's ideas regarding multiple intelligence; David Kolb's cycle of experiential learning which requires a shift 'towards teaching *how* to do something'; Daniel Goleman's seminal work on the impact of emotional intelligence on learning; and Paul Black and Dylan Wiliam's research on the impact of assessment for learning as an alternative to summative assessment. All have profound implications for the development of learning in our schools.

This has been identified in *2020 Vision: Report of the Teaching and Learning in 2020 Review Group* (2007), reporting on the requirements for personalising learning for Ofsted, which recommends that 'all children and young people leave school with functional skills in English and Maths, understanding how to learn, think creatively, take risks and handle change'.

What changes do we need to see in our schools?

A crucial requirement is to have a greater focus on *how* we learn and a determined drive to develop an educational system that helps children learn more effective life skills rather than learning 'stuff'.

This paradigm shift in emphasis should include developing in students a deep understanding of their own learning profiles and how to use these to raise achievement and develop their full potential. Teachers, students and parents all need to understand their learning styles and how to engage the brain and manage their minds for learning. Students could then use this knowledge to develop transferable skills, especially in literacy, numeracy, communication and self-management, in order to become the emotionally intelligent, flexible learners needed for the twenty-first century.

In addition, schools have to develop students' skills in teamwork and cooperation that are so evident in the activities children take part in outside of school, such as sports and productions. Extra-curricular activities have often been 'tacked on' to an overcrowded, content-dominated curriculum rather than being placed at the centre of a competency-based curriculum that focuses on skills acquired rather than information remembered.

Our students have to become more aware of their place in the world and become competent in building rapport with other cultures. It is likely they will work for international companies and communicate in a virtual environment where geography is no longer a barrier to communication. As the youngsters of the emerging nations, such as China and India, embrace the electronic era with a creativity and determination borne of cultural economic disadvantage, we must ensure that our future generations can compete.

From one teacher at age 10 to fourteen teachers at age 11?

The present models of a compartmentalised curriculum based on subject content, the teacher as an expert and the student as a passive recipient, have not produced the skills and competences our young people need to become successful learners. Almost fifty per cent are still deemed to 'fail' by not achieving the standard five A*–C GCSE target and more importantly employers worry that students move into work without the self-management skills they need for the workplace. A holistic approach to education that focuses on competences rather than curriculum, and emotional intelligence rather than notions of fixed IQ seems to be the essential learning paradigm for the next generation.

In England the Royal Society of Arts (RSA) Opening Minds curriculum for the encouragement of art, manufacturing and commerce is one such alternative model being adopted in schools with very promising outcomes, including improved motivation and a confident approach to independent learning. Combining this with a Learning to Learn/thinking skills approach could be a powerful model for twenty-first century curriculum planning. This combined approach can be delivered through projects that are mapped against curriculum objectives and include many cross-curricular links such as Citizenship, ICT and literacy. This model has been developed by the Qualifications and Curriculum Authority (QCA) through the personal, learning and thinking skills (PLTS), and this book uses these competences to develop the schemes and lessons for implementing such a curriculum. However, the principles of the RSA Opening Minds competency model form the basis for this approach to learning.

The present model in English schools is for students to move from primary schools, where they have one teacher, to a large organisation where up to fourteen teachers deliver separate subject specialisms. For 11–14-year-olds this can lead, at worst, to disengagement and, most commonly, a plateauing of progress. This is followed by an examination driven, content-heavy GCSE course for two years. Teachers have become expert at 'teaching to the test' to push up exam results and students often reach 16 years of age having learnt to become passive consumers of education and without the essential skills in literacy, numeracy, creativity and independent learning.

> *The improvement in school performance has been achieved by teachers working harder and often spoon-feeding students so that they can pass exams. Children need to work harder than teachers if they are to fulfil their potential!*
>
> **Head teacher**

A competency-based curriculum model can develop an academic curiosity and independence that allows students to take more responsibility for their own learning. Many schools have found that the opportunities provided by the more flexible KS3 curriculum provides opportunities for a radical shift in focus from teaching content to learning skills. Whether it is termed *themed learning*, *project-based learning* or a *competency curriculum*, the crucial difference is a change in

focus towards engaging students in active, rich learning experiences which develop the habits of self-management with a focus on teamwork to develop excellent communication skills.

> *We have to do extra work in Opening Minds but it doesn't feel like homework because I want to do it for the team. I've got so carried away with one project I am writing a book!*
>
> *Opening Minds has made me more independent and given me important skills of working in a team. We got to know our teacher really well because we weren't just seeing her once a week and this helped build our confidence.*
>
> **Student comments**

Schools have found that when delivering this type of lesson they become facilitators of and for learning, as well as subject specialists. The work produced has been impressive enough for schools to demonstrate improvements in standards, for example, in literacy levels and ultimately in exam results. One of the most powerful outcomes reported by schools is the impact on staff who have taught the course.

> *I was wary about teaching outside my subject area but when you see how the students are motivated and achieving so much more you realise it's about teaching students how to teach themselves.*
>
> **Opening Minds teacher in a high attaining school**
>
> *Teaching a competency-based course to Year 7 has given me a new lease of life for the conclusion of my career. I have seen our students make fantastic progress from their low literacy base and behaviour problems have disappeared.*
>
> **Teacher who introduced a competency-based approach in 2007 at a seriously challenged school**

Many schools have adopted various approaches to developing Learning to Learn over recent years ranging from training days to discrete courses for students and 'learning passports' to use across the curriculum. The approach conceived by Guy Claxton outlining the 5Rs—Reflectiveness, Resourcefulness, Responsibility, Reasoning and Resilience—has been used as a focus for several schools in developing their competency-based approach.

> *Some of the less engaged boys demonstrated a commitment to the task which was beyond expectations. Over the series of lessons learners were able to identify how the 5Rs attributes they were developing could be linked to their success in the adult world.*
>
> **Teacher delivering competency-based lessons to Year 8 class**

If the above curriculum changes are combined with a rigorous behaviour policy that focuses on choosing to learn and an active student voice programme that encourages a sense of ownership, enterprise and responsibility, the possibilities of engaging students in a learning culture becomes much more likely. If we supplement this with teaching the habits of emotional intelligence such as persistence, optimism and self-management across the curriculum, as suggested by the recommended Social and Emotional Aspects of Teaching and Learning (SEAL) initiative, then we are achieving the essential shift needed. This is the application of research evidence of brain-friendly ways to learn: active participation, variety and challenge and emotional involvement combine to make learning exciting but demanding. It's the way we are wired!

A crucial aspect of this new pedagogy is metacognition—reflective practice. Constant reflection about learning how and why it works is part of a competency-based curriculum. It is through this reflection that progress is assessed, reviewed and understood.

The organisation of the school environment must also reflect the need for flexible approaches that create individualised learning opportunities and provide a safe and inspiring backdrop to learning experiences. This flexibility would need to extend to the timetable, the school terms and of course the classrooms.

Summative assessment at given ages will need to be replaced by students travelling through their learning programmes as and when they are ready, with mixtures of ages in each class reflecting

a really individualised approach to progress. Embedding formative assessment for learning will help students to track their own progress through learning programmes centred on the development of competencies. This can be rigorously moderated by teachers or the other adults supporting their learning.

> *Paul Black and Dylan Wiliam demonstrated the double impact of assessment for learning: it improves scores in national tests and examinations as well as metacognitive skills, including the capacity to learn how to learn. Techniques such as open questioning, sharing learning objectives and success criteria, and focused marking have a powerful effect on the extent to which learners are enabled to take an active role in their learning.*
>
> **John Bransford, Ann Brown and Rodney Cocking, *How People Learn: Brain, Mind, Experience and School* (2000)**

Finally the whole culture of schooling could move towards one of active learning centres where the day is flexible and built around learning needs with extra-curricular activities as part of a package of opportunities and choices that build up a portfolio of competence that will profile achievement throughout school life.

Learning to Learn – what are schools doing now that works?

The extract below from the Demos report *About Learning* (2005) examines work in English schools that have successfully implemented a Learning to Learn agenda and thereby improved results. This is useful because it underpins any ethos that develops a competency-based curriculum. Such schools have:

- *A passion for learning is central to their work; teachers and learners have a shared and agreed understanding of what effective learning is. Learning infuses the organisation and directs its improvement agenda. All aspects of life in school or college are underpinned by the* question 'how will this impact on learning in this place?' In some schools a discrete Learning to Learn course explicitly develops the habits, dispositions and attitudes to support learning; in other schools a similar approach is diffused across the curriculum.

■ This passion for learning leads the staff to be constantly looking outward for ideas and schemes that will advance the quality of teaching and learning in the school/college. They will test these new developments, sometimes with a small group that conducts trials and experiments, then discarding practices that do not work but adopting and sharing more widely those that do.

■ Classrooms are learner-centred. Close attention is paid to the knowledge, skills and attitudes which the learner brings into the classroom. Learning is connected to what is already known and misconceptions are identified, explored and corrected. Students assume an active role in all aspects of learning, including creating their own hypotheses, setting their own questions, coaching one another, setting goals for themselves, monitoring progress, experimenting with ideas and taking risks knowing that mistakes are an inherent part of learning. The flow of work is sufficiently varied and challenging to maintain the students' engagement but not so difficult as to lead to discouragement. This engagement gives opportunities for students of all abilities to succeed and avoid the disaffection and attention-seeking from peers that gives rise to behaviour management problems.

■ Classrooms are knowledge-centred in that they encourage deep learning as opposed to shallow learning. An observer in such classrooms sees students contributing thought-provoking comments, posing probing questions and proposing solutions to problems while analysing the ideas of others as well as their own. Students are encouraged and supported to take risks in their learning and to see 'being stuck' as a learning opportunity.

■ In assessment-centred classrooms, assessment is both formative and summative and becomes a tool to aid learning: students monitor their progress over time and with their teachers identify the next steps needed to improve. Techniques such as open questioning, sharing learning objectives and focused marking have a powerful effect on students' ability to take an active role in their learning. There is always sufficient time left for reflection by students. Whether individually or in pairs, students are given the opportunity to review what they have learnt and how they have learnt it. They evaluate themselves and one another in a way that contributes to understanding. Students know their levels of achievement and make progress towards their next goal.

> The illiterate of the 21st century will not be those who cannot read and write, but those who cannot learn, unlearn, and relearn.
>
> **Alvin Toffler, *Rethinking the Future* (1996)**

Students do not learn in isolation. There is a deliberately created *learning community* in which both staff and students think of themselves as learners. Students are encouraged to help and support one another and to collaborate in a spirit of intellectual camaraderie. They work in groups with attention paid to listening skills, body language, techniques of respectful disagreement and so on. The ethos is characterised by mutual respect and the development of the self-management needed for resilience in learning, and it culminates in the creation of independent, reflective learners for life.

Such schools and colleges adjust the organisation of the day or week and reconfigure the timetable to provide experiences that strengthen student learning and motivation. There is the flexibility to create blocks of time for learning projects, off-site learning or real-life experience, as well as structured enrichment programmes through clubs and sports.

Such schools and colleges also engage with the wider community through workshops on learning for parents and governors. A website offers the online curriculum with access for parents and students to all schemes, lesson plans, extension tasks and success criteria, so that the home–school link becomes a powerful tool for extending the learning experience.

The staff ensure that their students enjoy their learning and become confident and independent in learning. The teachers' focus on learning means that in their classrooms the art of teaching meets the science of learning.

The above examples of great practice show what schools are doing to create the 'learning' school of the future which will prepare our young people for the challenges ahead.

What innovations do we need to introduce and what should we abandon in our institutions to create the 'learning' school?

The following table is not an exhaustive list but suggests some ideas for what we could innovate and abandon in our schools system in order to develop a configuration of education that creates young people who will be successful citizens for 2020. This model can be used for developing ideas in different school contexts.

Preparing students for the 21st century	Innovate	Abandon
KS2–3 transition (11 years)	Transfer when ready Teachers who can teach in primary and secondary schools Phased transition	Transfer when 11 Primary and secondary qualifications which exclude the ability to teach in each phase Transition in September
KS3 Curriculum (11–14 years)	A competency-based curriculum for KS3 based on projects mapped against National Curriculum skills required for subjects, preferably taught by one teacher Encourage the transference of skills. Introduce Maths/Science/Technology-based projects and English/Humanities/Arts-based projects with only Modern Foreign Languages and PE taught discretely Embed communication skills including literacy and numeracy in cross-curricular projects Develop some subject specialism through KS3 to prepare for the 14–19 phase. Take KS3 SATs and GCSEs when students are ready. Students of varying ages will study together depending on progress made	Up to 14 separate subjects from Year 7 delivered for one hour or more a week by 14 different teachers The compartmentalisation of the curriculum in secondary schools which can restrict the ability to transfer skills and competences and impede the embedding of learning Attempts to manage literacy and numeracy across the curriculum in secondary schools with paid posts Students grouped by age rather than stage of learning
Timetables	Flexible timetables with blocks of time for project or themed work	Fixed timetables divided into up to one hour periods from 9–4 p.m.

Preparing students for the 21st century	Innovate	Abandon
Assessment	Rigorous student-led assessment for learning through KS2–4 using data available and tracking tools to target underachievers	Summative testing and school league tables
	Develop a portfolio of achievements and competences in KS2–4 to include extra-curricular activities and levels of attainment in a variety of subjects with a diploma awarded	Up to 11 GCSEs taken at 16 with no accreditation for extra-curricular achievements
Engaging learners	Establish the ethos and belief in all schools that intelligence can be learnt and that there are a variety of ways to be clever	Notions of fixed IQ
	Train teachers to be aware of the optimal environmental conditions for learning: stress-free, praise focused and creatively challenging	Controlling rather than motivating classrooms
	Train students to take responsibility for their own learning through an understanding of how to learn and having responsibility for their learning	Students expecting to be entertained and spoon-fed for the exam
	Use assessment for learning and peer/self-assessment techniques to give students a true understanding of how to progress	Summative grades that neither motivate nor assist progress in learning
	Create a learning environment that works with the brain in mind and which facilitates peripheral learning	Classrooms built for chalk and talk with the teacher as the font of all knowledge talking at the students
	Use novelty, variety, humour, colour, challenge and music which all appeal to the emotional brain and have clear, consistent, high expectations to motivate students	Inconsistent delivery of boring subject content through working from textbooks or copying from the board
	Create positive relationships using a behaviour policy that describes what we want and applies sanctions consistently	The tolerance of bad behaviour that impacts on the learning opportunities of others
	Underpin all lessons with the development of emotional intelligence to include persistence, self-awareness, self-management, optimism and deferred gratification to produce resilient learners	The notion that exists amongst some students and parents that students can achieve without determination and hard work

cont.

9

Preparing students for the 21st century	Innovate	Abandon
Creating independent learners for life and responsible, productive citizens of the global community	Self-management through emotional intelligence to underpin all KS3–4 courses	Teachers 'towing' students through the tests at KS2–4 thereby disempowering them and preventing them from becoming independent learners
	Students taught life skills such as Citizenship, an understanding of the brain and their learning styles. Embed life skills, enterprise and ICT within the project-based curriculum at KS3	PSHE and Citizenship tacked on to the overloaded National Curriculum
	All students to have handheld ICT devices for use at school and at home across the curriculum	Classrooms and lesson dedicated to ICT
	Teamwork and cooperation encouraged with accreditation for group activity inside and outside the classroom	Only individual achievement is assessed and accredited

Summary of points

■ Schools need to develop skills and competences in self-management and learning as well as subject knowledge.

■ We need to engage learners in early secondary education to take responsibility for their learning.

■ The flexible KS3 curriculum can offer opportunities to teach themed learning that teaches subjects in exciting contexts.

■ If we can help students to develop excellent independent learning habits, their progress through 14–19 pathways will be more successful.

■ The teacher's role may be enhanced by new approaches to pedagogy.

Useful reading

Beere, J., *The Key Stage 3 Learning Kit* (Sussex: Connect Publications, 2002).

Bransford, J. D., Brown, A. L. and Cocking, R. R. (eds.), *How People Learn: Brain, Mind, Experience and School* (Washington, DC: CBASSE, 2000).

Claxton, G., *Hare Brain, Tortoise Mind* (London: Fourth Estate, 1997).

Demos, *About Learning: Report of the Learning Working Group* (London: Demos, 2005).

Gilbert, C., *2020 Vision: Report of the Teaching and Learning in 2020 Review Group* (London: DfES, 2007).

Goleman, D., *Emotional Intelligence: Why It Can Matter More Than IQ* (London: Bloomsbury, 1996).

Middlewood, D., Parker, R. and Beere, J., *Creating a Learning School* (London: Paul Chapman, 2005).

Royal Society of Arts, *Opening Minds: Giving Young People a Better Chance* (London: RSA, 2005).

Toffler, A., and Gibson, R. (eds.), *Rethinking the Future* (London: Nicholas Brearley Publishing, 1996).

Wiliam, D. and Black, P., *Inside the Black Box* (London: NFER Nelson, 2006).

Chapter 2
How Can a Competency Curriculum Motivate Learners?

If we get the learning right, kids are too engaged to misbehave!

The competency-based curriculum is a new model of learning for KS3 which creates self-motivated students who achieve their potential.

In this chapter we will discuss:

- Why teenagers have all the potential motivation they could ever need to be excellent learners.

- Why we shouldn't keep doing what doesn't work at KS3.

- What changes we need to make to improve motivation and behaviour.

- How we can try to ensure that students of all abilities achieve everything they can.

- How we can use what we know about the brain to encourage a positive commitment to learning.

Young people are natural learners with bags of energy and curiosity. They are driven to learn what they need to know in order to survive and grow.

Does this sound like your students? Or do you have a class of sulky, apathetic, lethargic students who can't wait to get out of the classroom and who come to life only when the bell goes for breaktime?

Now think of babies when they are learning to walk. They are:

- Driven to get up on their feet and take ambitious scary steps into the unknown.

- Determined to keep trying—no matter how many times they fall over.

- Dogged in using every resource available to lever themselves onto their feet and have another go.

- Not embarrassed to wobble.

- Not afraid of looking silly.

Babies are single-minded and incredibly motivated to find a way. Have you seen the look of pure delight on their faces and the pleasure they take in success as they practise those first wobbly steps to freedom? If only our teenage students (and we!) could recapture that resilience and determination!

So how is it possible to bring that sort of motivation back into the hearts and minds of our teenagers? It is still there. They show massive persistence and motivation to learn about whatever matters to them and how to share it. The same applies to music, computer games, skateboarding tricks, football skills, learning to play for the school rock band and so on.

So what's wrong with our classrooms? Could it be a curriculum created for the industrial age built around subjects which aims to create leaders and workers? The development of the competency curriculum has been long anticipated:

The subject based curriculum will be seen much more as a means than an end. Education for understanding will become the focus with the emphasis on developing a rich portfolio of cognitive skills. The cognitive curriculum will become the basis for planning, delivering and assessing learning. The core purpose of education will be seen as the development of an autonomous learner whose success will be measured in terms of thinking skills founded on literacy and numeracy.

John West-Burnham,
The School of the Future (2000)

A KS3 school week in numbers …

Students may experience having up to 14 teachers per week, 10 subjects, 15 homework tasks, 6 ongoing projects, 2.5 hours of tutor time, 2 hours of assemblies, 2 hours of PE, 2 hours of tests, 2 hours queuing for dinner or tuck shop, at least 2.5 hours walking between classrooms at lesson change, 15 hours having to be 'quiet', 12 hours writing, 5 hours reading, 20 hours sitting on a hard chair, 12 hours listening and 2 hours a week with their hand up! Most of this time is directed and compulsory—and most teachers still do all of the talking.

The latest survey by Campaign for Learning in 2008 shows that copying and listening has actually increased in recent years in classrooms:

	2008	2007	2004	2003	2002
Copying from board or book (hours)	65	52	61	63	56
Listening to the teacher talking for a long time (hours)	63	33	39	37	37

Source: Ipsos MORI Young People Omnibus Survey (2008)

However, it's not always like this. As teachers we have all experienced those pure moments of 'flow' when the class really is in the palm of your hand and we've somehow made an almost spiritual connection. These moments occur when the learning has really connected together like a magic puzzle.

Outlined below are some of the features of a competency-based or themed curriculum which can motivate students and help recreate those magic moments more often.

What is a competency-based curriculum?

A competency-based curriculum is where the delivery focuses on outcomes related to competences rather than content. The traditional subject-based delivery is replaced in these lessons by a cross-curricular approach which links together many different specialisms to enhance learning. Content is delivered via a pedagogy that encourages active, independent learning through group-work and student-centred learning in which the teacher acts most often as a facilitator. This is in contrast to a didactic, teacher-led approach where the teacher dominates the discourse and asks the questions. The idea of a less didactic model of learning is not a new concept, as Jean Piaget observed in 1945: 'The principal goal of education is to create men [sic] who are capable of doing new things, not simply repeating what other generations have done—men who are creative, inventive and discoverers.'

The competency curriculum has been proposed by the Qualifications and Curriculum Authority (QCA) in response to a need to develop skills for employability known now as the personal, learning and thinking skills (PLTS) in which students are encouraged to become:

- Team workers
- Self-managers
- Independent enquirers
- Effective participators
- Reflective learners
- Creative thinkers

These skills can be taught through subjects but a competency approach at KS3 links subjects together and delivers the learning through themes or projects. These are completed by students under the supervision of teachers whose lesson objectives aim to develop and assess the competences rather than merely test the acquisition of a bank of knowledge. Many schools have delivered Learning to Learn as a first project, taught in the first half term for about six hours a week,

and in this way hope to develop an ownership and responsibility for learning in the hearts and minds of their students. Again, this is not a new concept. As Benjamin Bloom said in 1956: 'The purpose of education is to change the thoughts and feelings and actions of students.'

A competency curriculum thus first and foremost delivers competences and skills, usually within a project, delivered by a teacher who facilitates active learning experiences and who measures the successful acquisition of the competences. Much of this type of pedagogy is simply best practice for engaging learners and has often been observed in different subjects and on cross-curricular days. However, rearranging the delivery of subjects into cross-curricular projects offers an opportunity to take more radical steps towards engaging learners in active, independent learning.

Opening Minds is the name of the Royal Society of Art's competency curriculum and has its own set of competences that are delivered through a themed or project-based approach.

Real learning in an Opening Minds classroom

Imagine a classroom where all students are focused and buzzing with the excitement of learning. Some are sitting at laptops putting finishing touches to their PowerPoint presentation on Global Issues and sharing thoughts with their teacher about which animation looks most effective. Others are standing, practising a presentation with a large display of leaves and mosses stuck onto a massive poster. One or two are sitting flicking through their folders drawing together an evaluation of their competences, admiring the work they've done in this project and peer-assessing each others' work. A pair of students are discussing the research material they found on an internet search. A small group are sitting on the floor in the corner experimenting with a board game created to promote environmental awareness. One student is fixed in intense concentration creating a model from unbent paper clips and tape to use as a mini recycle centre. The noise is busy and lively and self-directed. For a moment I can't see where the teacher is. Then I realise the bell went five minutes ago—but nobody has moved ...

Where are we now?

'School is boring' is the most common criticism that comes from students whose achievement starts plateauing at Year 8. When students join secondary education they are keen to learn and spend lots of time straining to get attention and have a go with their hands in the air. There are lots of accompanying 'Oohhhs' as they try to be the person to attempt to answer the questions and get the praise.

In too many cases, that infectious enthusiasm turns into noisy disruption within a year. After two more years, students can become passive, dependent and even resistant to any independent learning, waiting instead for their teachers to tow them through Key Stage 4. But these same students can shine again when placed in a skateboarding park, in front of a computer game, under a car bonnet or when given ingredients to make cosmetics to prepare a friend's face for a party night.

To be motivated, students have to see the point of what they learn and the connections it has to other learning and to their lives. No matter how worthy we feel the content of the National Curriculum is, many of our students don't seem to agree. We need to make learning interesting, fun, connected with the students' lives and with their emotional brains.

> 'Dull lessons with too much teacher talk' is cited by student voice research at a Local Authority as a reason for persistent absence.

'I'll do it when I feel like it'

So, what makes us feel like learning or working? Leading researchers say that understanding learners' emotions is one of the keys to motivation. Emotions influence not only motivation but also selective attention, event interpretation, prediction, recall, decision making, problem solving and, of course, learning: 'By learning to manage our own emotions, we can stay better motivated to be at our best' (Jensen 1995).

Dr Paul Maclean (1978) suggested the notion of the three part or triune brain:

■ *The reptilian brain* – responsible for basic responses to the environment such as territorial and ritualistic behaviours and behaviours which help us to survive by being ready to fight, fly, flock or freeze if threatened.

■ *The emotional brain* – often called the limbic system which helps us lay down long-term memories. We need to switch this on if learning is to be memorable.

■ *The thinking brain* – found in the neocortex (the folded outer layers of the brain) which is responsible for thought, reasoning and other higher order thinking skills.

The problem in a conventional classroom is that students may feel threatened, even if only by the embarrassment of getting it wrong, and so can downshift into 'reptilian' behaviour which is non-compliant or even aggressive—especially if the teacher is controlling and dominant. There is, unfortunately, plenty of opportunity for these student behaviours in the teacher-led model we have in much of our secondary teaching. However, when the teacher knows the individual students better, has them for more hours in the week and plays the facilitator and coach rather than being the fount of all knowledge, there is less room for conflict and more time for engagement with learning. So it can be with competency-based teaching.

In competency-based teaching the teacher does not play the traditional role of chalk and talk. In competency-based lessons, the subject matter is the vehicle through which we as teachers develop the dispositions and behaviours we want. The teacher is not the 'sage on the stage' but the 'guide on the side', generating less conflict and more motivation. We need to think diff   y about content and delivery in order to engage the emotional brain for learning.

> **Campaign for Learning – State of the Nation Survey**
>
> Results from a survey in 2008 demonstrated developments over the last ten years in students' perceptions of how they learn and how they want to learn.
>
> How do students prefer to learn?
>
> 56% prefer practical (35% in 1998)
>
> 37% prefer computers
>
> 17% from a teacher (29% in 1998)
>
> How do students actually experience learning in school?
>
> 65% copy from board or book
>
> 63% listening to a teacher talking for a long time
>
> *(These scores had been steadily declining until shooting back up in 2008.)*

'All learning has an emotional base'

What engages the emotional brain? Drama, suspense and celebration do. The emotional brain loves novelty and originality instead of the same stale old diet. How often are students distracted by a few flakes of snow or a wasp in the room? But the strange paradox is that students also love to be part of something which feels comfortable and where they can feel confident.

What do we remember? We remember what makes an impact in our emotional brain—challenge, colour, enthusiasm, humour, mystery and intrigue, music, rhythm, rhyme and, of course, praise, maybe even love. A child will always work harder for the teacher they love and who loves them. But how can you create that sort of rapport with a child you see for only two hours a week?

What the brain needs for optimal motivation

We have made huge progress in our understanding of the brain and how learning works. The following points (drawn from the combined work of Singer et al. which is cited by Eric Jensen in *The Learning Brain* (1995)) identify some of the main features of how classrooms should feel and look, and which are now seen as essential for engagement with learning:

■ A degree of (student) control or choice over the learning taking place.

■ The learning must have some kind of relevance and meaning that is related to needs.

■ The learning must have distinctive, thematic, 'real world' contexts.

■ The learning environment must be risk-free, playful and safe.

■ Positive social bonding is a core element of the learning experience.

■ There should be flexible goals that are low stress and high challenge.

■ Hope—there must be a belief that the learning outcomes can be achieved.

Some of these factors are present some of the time in schools but a curriculum that is compartmentalised and lessons which are restricted by time, place and person make it hard for teachers to create the above conditions for learning. In addition, the reward and incentive schemes used in schools to create motivation can be counterproductive. A study by Teresa Amabile of Brandeis University (1989) found that long-term rewards just don't work—especially for creativity. Intrinsic enjoyment of learning for its own sake is much more productive (see also Alfie Kohn's *Punished by Rewards* (1999)).

> **IF**
>
> Challenge is greater than the skills = anxiety
>
> Skills are greater than the challenge = boredom
>
> Solution = match up skills and challenge
>
> How? By creating a flexible curriculum which links up the learning with the skills required

Research has shown that providing choice within learning is a crucial factor in creating motivation. When students are working on themed approaches in project lessons they are less likely to be involved in disconnected tasks like copying from the board, completing tests, worksheets and other things done 'to' them. Instead, they have a role within the group to produce materials on a long-term basis. They are encouraged to take responsibility for the success of the project and outcomes. Through assessment for learning they can monitor their progress against the objectives and competences. The lessons are longer and the projects are deeper because of the time available. Activities are more within the control of the students. Also, learners who tend to focus more on fun and friendship may be able to get more engaged when there are ample opportunities for self-determination and peer interaction.

Become an expert

Every child needs to become an expert in their own personal development. The competency-based curriculum puts that development at the heart of its assessment processes. The very first Learning to Learn project for many schools in Year 7 investigates aspects of the brain—how learning happens and the student's personal profile for learning. Establishing a language for describing yourself as a learner, and having self-assessment against the competencies as a regular activity, makes every student an expert in that most important aspect of learning—him or herself.

Self-awareness is the key to emotional intelligence and underpins success, self-discipline and resilience in learning. With emotional intelligence comes the ability to see learning as a reward in itself. The evidence from work in schools on a competency-based curriculum shows that motivation comes from an enjoyment of the joined up nature of the project work and the satisfaction gained from working in teams. The team approach also develops the empathy and communication skills which employers are demanding for careers in the service dominated industries.

Case study: Longfield School, Darlington

Longfield School in Darlington, County Durham, is an 11–16 secondary school with Sports College status. We have 930 students. Longfield is a school well equipped for the twenty-first century, where each student is encouraged to appreciate learning and to reach their potential.

Following a whole school curriculum review in 2006 involving students, staff, feeder primary staff, parents, governors and post-16 providers, we have introduced many changes to our curriculum. These changes have included major shifts in the way we deploy people, organise learners into groups and divide time.

In September 2007 we introduced a competency-based curriculum in Year 7 called Opening Minds (OM) based on the RSA scheme but we re-designed the curriculum to make it relevant to the school, topical issues and locality whilst still focusing on the competences developed by the RSA. In Year 7, all students follow the Opening Minds programme to allow more opportunities for deep learning. The flexibility of the timetable enables students to have eight hours per week of Opening Minds with one teacher in the same classroom. Time for this is organised with one full day and two blocks of two hours per week to allow for project-based work. This not only improves the efficiency of time use, it allows for students to work in a more focused and less fragmented way.

The reason for this innovation

Opening Minds was introduced to ease the transition between KS2 and KS3 and to ensure that our pupils are equipped with learning skills which will mean they can work collaboratively and independently with equal success. A school focus was to ensure higher order thinking skills were utilised from an early stage.

Many different competency-based curriculum models were considered by visiting and making links with organisations and schools. After visiting Campion School in Northampton we believed the RSA model would best suit the needs of our school, so in April 2006 planning started for eight hours per week of the Year 7 curriculum to be allocated to OM in which to teach a number of subjects through project-based lessons. Classrooms and staff were relocated to create an Opening Minds block and everyone felt out of their comfort zone at this stage! However, it was not long before schemes of work, lesson plans and resources were created and staff felt more confident about the delivery. Our projects included Longfield Life, Smart Brain, Dragon's Apprentice, Under Your Nose, Tomorrow's Rubbish, My Secret Life and a one-week outward bound project named Chariots of Fire in North Wales, in the snow!

Evidence of the impact of Opening Minds at Longfield

Feedback from both parents and pupils has been monitored to assess the impact of OM on transitional issues. In comparison to previous years pupils have had fewer problems and enjoy the process far more. Baseline testing was completed at the start and end of Year 7 relating to attitudes to learning, and formative formal assessment showed a jump in independent learning skills, creative thinking and resilience. Attendance figures improved and behaviour problems significantly decreased, particularly low level disruption. In comparison to previous years, pupils are now used to using a variety of strategies in order to complete a number of challenging tasks. Over the course of our first year of Opening Minds we had many visitors to the department, including governors, local head teachers and teachers from further afield who are also planning to introduce a competency-based curriculum. As Children's Commissioner, Professor Al Aynsley-Green commented after a visit: 'It is clear that the children feel like equal partners in how their school is run and I have no doubt that it is this sense of empowerment which helps to create such a positive and nurturing environment.'

Next steps in our journey

Our first year of Opening Minds at Longfield has been very busy but also very rewarding, and due to its success we have just introduced Opening Minds to Year 8 pupils. The main focus will be to continue working with the competences through Global Citizenship projects, developing our links with partner schools in Russia, Holland and La Reunion and to address many of the topical issues facing our learners in the twenty-first century.

Susan Johnson
Assistant Head Teacher
sjohnson@longfield.darlington.sch.uk

Within the competency-based curriculum the focus on developing the skills of emotional intelligence—self-awareness, self-esteem, self-discipline, empathy and optimism—can provide a backdrop to the subject matter that links everything with real life. For example, in a project entitled Global Affairs, a poem about refugees is assessed on empathy as well as on writing skills. In the same way, a common sense linking up of History with English and ICT through a task such as presenting a PowerPoint presentation about the importance of human rights past and present, would be an example of synergistic subject linking.

A competency-based curriculum offers more choice as the students learn how to make decisions about how to approach activities and who will do what within the group. The teacher facilitates, offering advice and guidance and handing over the leadership to the students, intervening only when coaching is needed to make students feel more empowered.

Homework at KS3 seems to be the one universally despised element of secondary school education—by the students who do it, the teachers who have to mark it, the parents who have to nag about it and by the head teachers who have to hear complaints about either too much or too little of it.

Homework has become an anachronism as more and more students do it (if at all!) in after-school sessions or in the lunch hour or during registration or copy it from the internet. However, a competency-based curriculum provides a great opportunity to make 'homework' into 'my work' or, better still, 'our work'. Parents have reported that students want to do homework based on projects because 'We've got to get it done by tomorrow for the group'. Students often develop their work way beyond the original teacher expectations—both in academic quality and in investment of the students' own time. Students often ask to stay on after school to complete group tasks. The main motivators are group loyalty and the feeling the students have that they are taking more control in setting their work, assigning tasks and monitoring their own and each others' performances. Students are often much stricter with each other and themselves in this regard than we would ever

be with them. This approach can appeal to the competitive instinct of boys and the communication imperative for girls.

Finally, feedback from the competency-based curriculum has shown that not only does it raise achievement through motivating students but it also develops confidence and self-esteem. Crucially it is motivational because it engenders hope—a competency-based curriculum really can foster a belief that learning outcomes can be achieved. This is true for all abilities from the Gifted and Talented to those with special needs, from the socially adept to the socially challenged.

> *I don't really like working with people but Opening Minds has made me feel more confident and motivated.*
>
> **Year 7 student**
>
> *I like doing this because it's much more interesting, fun and I make more decisions about how I do it.*
>
> **Year 8 student**

Summary of points

■ KS3 has traditionally led to an achievement plateau and deterioration in behaviour.

The competency-based curriculum approach works to motivate because:

■ The model of teaching in a competency-based curriculum is more about 'coaching' and facilitating and less about controlling.

■ Students have more control and choice over their learning tasks and their progress through the competences, so motivation is higher.

■ Competency-based curricula engage the emotional brain—learning can become more memorable through having greater social interaction, challenge, relevance, creativity and longer periods of time with projects and teachers.

■ Competency-based curricula link learning to the students' 'real world' by connecting the learning across subjects and to the wider world and to their own personal development.

■ The projects create a commitment which integrates work at home with work at school alleviating the persistent conflict over homework at school and at home.

■ The emphasis on group work creates an enjoyment and social bonding that makes learning memorable and encourages self-discipline and commitment.

■ Students see fewer teachers and less compartmentalisation of the curriculum which helps join up their learning.

■ Relationships with teachers are better as they see more of the students and so develop an intimate knowledge of their progress and needs.

■ With a competency-based curriculum there is less movement and less wasted time.

Useful reading

Amabile, T. M., *Growing Up Creative* (New York: Crown Publishing, 1989).

Beare, H. *Creating the Future School* (London: Routledge/Falmer, 2001).

Bloom, B. et al, *Brain, Mind and Behaviour* (New York: W.H. Freeman and Co, 1988).

Jensen, E, *The Learning Brain*, (San Diego, CA: Turning Point, 1995).

John, A., *Punished by Rewards: The Trouble with Gold Stars, Incentive Plans, A's, Praise, and Other Bribes* (Boston, MA: Houghton Mifflin, 1999).

Piaget, J., *Play, Dreams and Imitation in Childhood* (London: Heineman, 1945).

MacLean, P. D. *The Triune Brain in Evolution: Role in Paleocerebral Functions* (New York: Plenum Press, 1990).

West-Burnham, J. *The School of the Future* (Headlines, 2000).

Useful websites

www.openingminds.org.uk

www.thersa.org

Chapter 3
Delivering and Assessing a Competency-based Curriculum

It's up to you!

This chapter aims to:

- Give you ideas for delivering a competency-based curriculum within your school.

- Give you examples of models of delivery.

- Give you examples of progression levels which can be adapted for use in your school.

- Show the importance of involving students and staff in their formulation.

The key difference between a subject-based curriculum and a competency-based curriculum is that our objective is not only to allow students to acquire subject knowledge and skills but also make progress on the key competences. By measuring progress in these, and tracking students, we can ensure that this approach to learning has rigour. Traditional subject content will also be delivered and progress can be measured against the National Curriculum criteria if desired.

The competences you choose to measure should be chosen according to the context of the school. Key questions to ask at the outset are (amongst others):

- Do our students need to be more independent, creative or resilient?

- Should literacy and numeracy be at the heart of our competency-based curriculum?

- What are the strengths and weaknesses in our teaching and learning?

- What is our vision and what are our values and how can we build these into our curriculum?

Your focus for the competences will give you the criteria against which you can measure the progress of your students. You can see examples of these criteria later in this chapter. The skills and attitudes engendered in a competency-based curriculum are quite hard to measure, but are absolutely essential for success, so putting them at the centre of planning, assessing and delivery is vital if you are to make a powerful difference.

You can take any subject and put it together with others to deliver the competences in a themed learning experience or in a project-based approach delivered in larger chunks of time during particular weeks of the school year. A project or module on the Olympic Games, for example, may include National Curriculum content from Maths, Science, English, ICT, Art, History, Religious Studies and so on. But these would be linked together in such a way as to optimise and reinforce learning. It would be wise to plan projects to include vital skills and content from National Curriculum programmes. Examples of these links can be seen in the projects in this book.

A combination of the above approaches has been successful in some pilot schools. However, the most radical departures from the traditional compartmentalised curriculum have been the most powerful catalysts for change.

> *The original premise [of the RSA Opening Minds research group] that the National Curriculum was acting as a block to the development and realisation of the potential of our students has been proven.*
>
> **Patrick Hazlewood, *Marlborough School*. RSA Opening Minds Project (2005)**

Methods of delivery

Project-based learning can be delivered through:

1. Timetabled teaching time:
   Blocked days: Your competency curriculum is taught on certain whole days during the year.
   Blocked weeks: Your competency curriculum is taught for a whole week each term.
   Timetabled lessons: Your competency curriculum is set into your normal timetable, alongside other subjects.
   Carousel timetable: Your competency timetable is delivered for part of the term as part of a carousel delivery, where students move from one subject to another within the school year.

2. Tutor time or PSHE/Citizenship lessons.

3. Subject lessons across the curriculum, using competency-based objectives in addition to subject content objectives.

An example of how a twenty-five hour week could be planned for KS3 is shown in the following table:

	1	2	3	4	5	6	7	8	9	10	11	12	13	14	15	16	17	18	19	20	21	22	23	24	25
7	2 competency-based projects of 6 hours each per week. Humanities/Art and Design themes and ICT integral												Active Science					PE/ Health		MFL/ Literacy			Maths		
8	1 competency project for 6 hours a week co-designed by students to assess the competences and cover new curriculum material from English and Humanities						Arts		Science				Maths					PE/ Health		MFL/ Literacy			D and T/ ICT		
9	1 competency-based project lesson leading to Level 1/2 extended project (0.5 GCSE)						Science				Maths				Art and Design		Hums	Perf Arts		MFL			English		

Which competences?

Competences is the word we have chosen to describe the skills and attributes we think students need for twenty-first century living. The Royal School of Arts (RSA) competency-based framework is CLIPS:

C itizenship
L earning
I nformation handling
P eople – managing relationships
S ituation management

The aims of the curriculum as published by the Qualifications and Curriculum Authority (QCA) in 2008 are to create: successful learners, confident individuals and responsible citizens.

Competences could be attached to these three aims as shown below:

Successful learners 'Learning to Learn'	(Self-) Confident individuals 'Personal development'	Responsible citizens 'Citizenship'
Communication	Self-belief	Participation
Enquiry	Self-awareness	Enterprise and initiative
Creativity	Self-management	Global awareness
Independence	Interpersonal skills	Prepared for work
Resilience		Respect and integrity
Persistence		
Engagement		

The 5Rs competences developed by Guy Claxton (1997) offer further insights into the dispositions needed by twenty-first century learners: Resilience, Resourcefulness, Responsibility, Readiness and Reflectiveness.

You may already be using a set of competences such as the 5Rs and decide to use this framework as teachers already have experience with it. If this is the model you choose to use, the table below shows some ideas for criteria for progression in the 5Rs:

Level	Resilience	Resourcefulness	Responsibility	Readiness	Reflectiveness
Poor	■ Gives up easily ■ Holds back from participation	■ Dependent on help ■ Awaits solutions ■ Low self-belief	■ Requires constant supervision ■ Easily influenced	■ Does not plan or prepare ■ Not interested in making connections	■ Does not plan or prepare ■ Not interested in making connections
Average	■ Will try but can be distracted ■ Tends to be positive	■ Knows own learning preferences ■ Remembers well	■ Needs prompting to engage ■ Completes tasks	■ Will progress when prompted ■ Keen to learn when interested	■ Can be objective ■ Is tolerant and empathetic
Excellent	■ Is reluctant to give up ■ Enjoys a challenge	■ Excellent questioning skills ■ High self-belief	■ Gives and receives feedback ■ Is self-motivated	■ Eager to learn ■ Plans ahead ■ Practises regularly ■ Prepared to be challenged	■ Values diversity ■ Can manage change ■ Curious, with wide range of interests

(Guy Claxton's 5Rs model has been used by the Campaign for Learning in a research project led by Newcastle University and is an important aspect of the Alite L2L programme.)

The PLTS

The personal, learning and thinking skills introduced by QCA have evolved from the competences above and offer us perhaps the most comprehensive set of competences. One advantage of using the PLTS is that students in KS4 who are taking diplomas will be using them as part of their assessment model, so this creates consistency. It may be that some projects have more of a focus on one or two of the competences and this will need to be made clear to the students.

The PLTS are:

■ Teamworking

■ Self-management

■ Independent enquiry

■ Effective participation

■ Reflective learning

■ Creative thinking

The PLTS are described in the following terms on the QCA website (http://www.qca.org/uk):

Teamworkers

Focus:

Young people work confidently with others, adapting to different contexts and taking responsibility for their own part. They listen to and take account of different views. They form collaborative relationships, resolving issues to reach agreed outcomes.

Young people:

- collaborate with others to work towards common goals

- reach agreements, managing discussions to achieve results

- adapt behaviour to suit different roles and situations, including leadership roles

- show fairness and consideration to others

- take responsibility, showing confidence in themselves and their contribution

- provide constructive support and feedback to others.

Independent enquirers

Focus:

Young people process and evaluate information in their investigations, planning what to do and how to go about it. They take informed and well-reasoned decisions, recognising that others have different beliefs and attitudes.

Young people:

- identify questions to answer and problems to resolve, plan and carry out research, appreciating the consequences of decisions

- explore issues, events or problems from different perspectives

- analyse and evaluate information, judging its relevance and value, considering the influence of circumstances, beliefs and feelings on decisions and events

- support conclusions, using reasoned arguments and evidence.

Self-managers

Focus:

Young people evaluate their strengths and limitations, setting themselves realistic goals with criteria for success. They monitor their own performance and progress, inviting feedback from others and making changes to further their learning.

Young people:

- assess themselves and others, identifying opportunities and achievements

- set goals with success criteria for their development and work

- review progress, acting on the outcomes

- invite feedback and deal positively with praise, setbacks and criticism

- evaluate experiences and learning to inform future progress

- communicate their learning in relevant ways for different audiences.

Reflective learners

Focus:

Young people organise themselves, showing personal responsibility, initiative, creativity and enterprise with a commitment to learning and self-improvement. They actively embrace change, responding positively to new priorities, coping with challenges and looking for opportunities.

Young people:

- seek out challenges or new responsibilities and show flexibility when priorities change

- work towards goals, showing initiative, commitment and perseverance

- organise time and resources, prioritising actions

- anticipate, take and manage risks

- deal with competing pressures, including personal and work-related demands

- respond positively to change, seeking advice and support when needed

- manage their emotions, and build and maintain relationships.

Effective participators

Focus:

Young people actively engage with issues that affect them and those around them. They play a full part in the life of their school, college, workplace or wider community by taking responsible action to bring improvements for others as well as themselves.

Young people:

- discuss issues of concern, seeking resolution where needed

- present a persuasive case for action

- propose practical ways forward, breaking these down into manageable steps

- identify improvements that would benefit others as well as themselves

- try to influence others, negotiating and balancing diverse views to reach workable solutions

- act as an advocate for views and beliefs that may differ from their own.

Creative thinkers

Focus:

Young people think creatively by generating and exploring ideas, making original connections. They try different ways to tackle a problem, working with others to find imaginative solutions and outcomes that are of value.

Young people:

- generate ideas and explore possibilities

- ask questions to extend their thinking

- connect their own and others' ideas and experiences in inventive ways

- question their own and others' assumptions

- try out alternatives or new solutions and follow ideas through

- adapt ideas as circumstances change.

How do we assess a competency-based curriculum?

Assessment for learning incorporates formative assessment techniques. These are entirely appropriate for a competency-based curriculum. Self- and peer-assessment can be crucial aspects of a competency-based curriculum. These improve both the self-awareness of students and support the development of their personal skills. However, to be able to successfully self- and peer-assess, students need to know the criteria against which they are being judged for each competence.

It is the authors' experience that tracking six competences may be rather complicated for students. In the following table, the six PLTS have been merged into three related groups to simplify assessment for KS3.

The descriptions of typical traits (in normal type) and personal statements (in italics) demonstrate, in a qualitative way, the behaviours and habits we are working on or seeking through our competency objectives. The descriptions can be developed and added to by students and teachers as they evolve in your school. The use of bronze, silver and gold gives an opportunity to identify levels of achievement and perhaps allow you to give awards for achieving elements of golden learning at appropriate times. These competences can be endorsed in PSHEE and across all the other subjects by using some of the statements as objectives alongside subject objectives in lessons.

Using the PLTS to become a golden learner–some indicators of levels of progress

PLTS – typical traits	Bronze/Developing	Silver/Progressing	Gold/Mastering
Personal skills ■ **Team workers** ■ **Effective participators**	Reluctant to participate	Will participate in an activity	Flexible as a leader or participator in a group and will make the group have a successful outcome
	'I'm not interested in this'	*'I like working in groups'*	
	Lacks motivation to complete work tasks or to get involved in teamwork	Can make a good contribution to a team	*'My aim is that our group does well on the project'*
	'I find it hard to get on with others'	*'I listen to other people's opinions'*	Is conscious of sustainable solutions and international issues
	Doesn't always communicate in a respectful way to others or demonstrate empathy or tolerance	Has a sensitivity to global issues and international awareness	*'I think and care a lot about how I can help solve issues in the world'*
	'I only want to work with my friends'	*'I care about the rest of the world'*	Demonstrates self-respect and tolerance, empathy and respect for others
	Lacks awareness or concern regarding global issues	Respects others and can be trusted	*'People get on with me and I know how to get on with all sorts of different people'*
	'I don't really care about other people in the world'	*'I want to do the right thing'*	Has the confidence to generate enterprise ideas and follow them through
	Has not considered future working life	Has goals for future working life	*'I'm always thinking of ideas and projects'*
	'I don't know what I want to do when I grow up'	*'I want to work hard and do well in the future'*	Excellent communicator
	Low self-esteem	Has some involvement in extra-curricular activity or other interests	*'I'm good at talking about or presenting ideas to others'*
	'I'm no good at this'	*'I take part in a club at school and am interested in the news'*	Has goals and ambitions for working life
	Needs prompting to work effectively with others		*'I know just what I want to be in the future—even if it changes each week!'*
	'I get fed up trying to work with others and lose my temper easily'		Takes part in a wide range of school and home activities
	Limited interests		*'I have a variety of hobbies and interests'*
	'I have no hobbies'		

cont.

27

PLTS – typical traits	Bronze/Developing	Silver/Progressing	Gold/Mastering
Learning skills ■ **Self-managers** ■ **Reflective learners**	Finding out about themselves as a learner *'I never think about how I learn best'* Heavily dependent on one learning style *'I am a kinaesthetic learner so get bored listening'* Needs to ask for help to support learning *'I don't ask for help'* Gives up without thinking *'It's just too hard and I don't care'* Relies on teacher/coach for motivation *'I only work when I am told to'* Communication is less well developed *'I can't say or write what I mean'* Lack of self-awareness regarding skills and abilities *'I don't know what I'm good at'* Easily influenced *'I follow my mates' behaviour'* Easily bored and distracted	Knows own learning profile *'I know how I learn best'* Learns in various ways *'I am learning to use my brain in various ways'* Is interested in learning *'I want to know how to improve'* Willing to try out new ideas *'Making mistakes is an important part of learning'* Needs some support but will work independently *'I sometimes need help but will try first to do it'* Can communicate orally and in writing at a satisfactory level *'I can get my ideas across to others in writing'* Can reflect on their learning and how it can improve *'I make lists of things I have to do'*	Keen to volunteer *'I have volunteered to help out in my community'* Supports the achievement of others *'I believe I can do anything I set my mind on but most of all I want to help other people'* Knows learning profile and extends/applies it at all opportunities *'I know I can learn to be more clever if I work hard enough'* Enjoys the challenge of learning in various ways *'I like a challenge as it makes me learn more'* Never gives up but continues to try new approaches *'I really learn from making mistakes'* Can talk about their own learning and continuously reflect on it *'I know how I learn best and always think about how to be better'* Learns from mistakes *'If something doesn't work then I try a different way then a different way, until it works'* High self-esteem *'I know I am a good learner'*

Personal skills ■ **Team workers** ■ **Effective participators**	'I can't see the point in learning so I mess about and rarely finish my work' Needs help with organising time and resources 'I have no idea of the timetable and have lost all my pens'	Able to learn from mistakes with support 'I can work out how to improve my work with some help' Aware of abilities and skills and able to use them most of the time 'I know my weaknesses and strengths' Can organise time to complete most tasks to deadline 'I bring the right stuff to lessons and get most of my work done on time' Communicates well with peers 'I can explain what I've done to others'	Confident self-belief 'I believe I can do anything if I try hard enough' Welcomes constructive criticism 'I like getting feedback about how I am doing so that I can improve' Well organised and effective 'I always have a plan' Manages anxiety and challenges very well 'I am not afraid to try new things' Can gain excellent rapport with a variety of audiences 'I am able to speak confidently to all sorts of audiences' Can create useful states for learning 'I know what it takes to get me ready for learning'
Thinking skills ■ **Creative thinkers** ■ **Independent enquirers**	Reluctant to try new ideas 'I don't like thinking too much' Dependent upon teacher for confidence 'I prefer to be told what to do' Needs prompting to think 'I can't think of ideas easily' Finds visualising difficult 'I can't do it' Accepts instruction without question 'I can't see how to do it' Reactive rather than proactive 'I can't be bothered'	Sometimes produces good ideas 'I can think of ideas and get others to help me' Asks questions when prompted 'I will ask questions to help me with my work' Often able to work on own initiative 'I like to work on my own sometimes' Willing to try out new ways of working 'I enjoy new situations and meeting new people' Enjoys reading and investigating 'I like to read up about things I am learning'	Endlessly curious 'I like to work out why as well as how' Asks difficult questions and challenges concepts 'I like asking difficult questions' Can process information effectively from a variety of sources 'I like to try many different solutions until I get it right' Capable of original thinking 'I always have lots of ideas'

cont.

PLTS – typical traits	Bronze/Developing	Silver/Progressing	Gold/Mastering
	Finds metacognition a challenge *'I don't like to be different'*	Can cope well with change *'When something unexpected happens I can adapt my responses'* Learning to manage memory and thinking *'I have techniques for learning things that help me remember'* Interested in new ideas *'I like to try new things and new ways of learning'*	Produces many creative ideas *'I get very involved in my projects and usually go off in new directions'* Uses own initiative to develop beyond expectation *'I get on with my work and often do things that the teacher didn't ask for'* Breaks the rules for good reasons *'I have my own individual style'* Powerful determination to find imaginative solutions *'I believe there is no limit to how much I can learn'*

The PLTS model is the one we have used later in this book to set objectives for lessons and measure progress. The Tracker Pack (see Section 4) can be used by both student and teacher to keep track of progress. The pack will provide evidence of self and teacher assessment in the competences and evidence of progression. It also therefore allows opportunities for reporting and rewards. It could become the equivalent of a learning passport and may be recorded in student planners and diaries. If the competences are to be delivered in other subjects as well as the project-based lessons, then the Tracker Pack can be used to monitor progress across the whole curriculum.

Displaying the competences for daily reference

The progress model above can be produced as a classroom display for maximum impact. When this is done, schools have found that students identify the level they are working at more easily, and can better identify the formative assessment criteria we measure ourselves by on a regular basis.

In addition, it is recommended that the English Speaking and Listening Assessment of Pupil Progress (APP) models are used during the delivery of the projects. (http://nationalstrategies. standards.dcsf.gov.uk/node/16051.) This type of learning lends itself very well to the development of speaking and listening skills as there can be lots of teamwork and presentation work. This adds an additional set of criteria for students and teachers to measure their progress against. Development of these communication skills is completely within the spirit of a competency-based curriculum.

Finally, all of the above will be reinforced by introducing the PLTS as a school-wide initiative across all the subjects and years and supported within the Advice and Guidance provision. If teachers use a PLTS objective in addition to their subject objective, the message will be reinforced in a very powerful way for all learners. As the PLTS are then built into schemes of work and delivered by teachers regularly they will become really useful learning 'habits' which will make a major contribution to school improvement.

> *It's good to know what we are aiming for so that we can keep remembering what learning is all about.*
>
> *We focus on one of the competences for each week and then we think about how we are developing it.*
>
> **Student comments**

> *I was sceptical but it's changed the way I think and it's given these children a different view of themselves as learners, as well as a massive boost in their empathy, social skills and their core skills. Also I am a better teacher, more open and re-energised.*
>
> **Lead teacher in competency class**

Students becoming independent learners

During the delivery of the competency curriculum in Year 7 it is hoped that students will acquire a language for learning and a sense of the required habits for learning which they can take into Year 8. If students develop this language then it follows that the projects have more student input in their design and outcomes. This can be seen in the Breakthrough Projects in Section 3. By Year 9, students can complete an independent project which uses all the skills they have acquired. This can then be an opportunity to gain half a GCSE (project level 1 or 2: AQA or Edexcel) and demonstrate by external accreditation how they have progressed with the competences. (www.edexcel.com/quals/projects/ www.aqa.org.uk/over/extendedprojectpoints/)

Summary of points

■ It is important to consider the aims and content of your competency framework, so that it best suits the students in your school.

■ A competency-based curriculum aims to deliver skills and competences, in addition to traditional knowledge and content.

■ A competency-based curriculum can be delivered in various ways, from whole days or weeks out of regular timetable, to regular timetabled blocks or across the curriculum in subjects.

■ Competences can also be reinforced in PSHE and Citizenship lessons and in assemblies and form tutor periods.

■ A competency framework can be delivered in all subjects across the curriculum as well as in project-based lessons.

■ It is crucial to create a progression model which will enable you and the students themselves to track progress in the competences across time and topic.

■ Use the English Speaking and Listening APP model as an additional measure of progress—particularly if literacy and self-confidence are important issues for your school.

■ Students should move through Year 7 to a more independent approach so that they are co-designing their projects by Year 8 and undertaking an accredited independent project by Year 9.

■ A Tracker Pack or passport owned by the student may be a good way of monitoring progress in the competences for teachers, parents and students. However, electronic methods can also be used by teachers and students to track progress over time in the different competences.

■ Extensive training for staff and students in the competences will ensure the successful impact of the competency approach.

■ Recognise and reward progress in the competences through special achievement evenings and events and external accreditation.

Useful reading

Claxton, G., *Hare Brain, Tortoise Mind* (London: Fourth Estate, 1997).

Hazlewood, P., *Marlborough School: Nurturing Independent Thinkers*. RSA Opening Minds Project (Stafford: Network Educational Press, 2005).

Useful websites

www.edexcel.com/quals/project
www.aqa.org.uk/over/extendedproject

Case study: Cheslyn Hay Sports and Community High School, Walsall

Our starting point was a recognition that although many of our students were arriving in the sixth form with good GCSE results, not enough were arriving with sufficiently developed attributes and thinking skills which would help them survive the demands of AS and A2 and then thrive in a university environment far removed from school.

One solution for us was to focus on developing the attributes of responsibility, resilience, reflectiveness, reasoning and resourcefulness (the 5Rs) through a coherent whole school process. This is accompanied by the delivery of Learning to Learn lessons for Years 7 and 8 to support their learning across the curriculum.

This approach includes:

- introducing teachers to the notion of the 5Rs as attributes which need developing explicitly in learners

- asking teachers to include a 5R objective in their planning and to share this with learners

- encouraging teachers to use the 5R terminology in their discussions with learners and in written reports

- ensuring learners hear and see the terminology in a wider school context via assemblies, classroom displays and use of their planners

- encouraging teachers to include opportunities for reflection on learning progress, identification of 5R strengths and weaknesses and 5R target-setting in their lesson planning

- rewarding learners demonstrating 5Rs both within and outside the classroom

- informing teachers about the skills and knowledge developed in Learning to Learn lessons so that they can provide opportunities for learners to demonstrate them in their lessons.

Hand in hand with developing the 5R attributes is the importance of developing learner motivation. We were lucky to be involved in the QCA project focusing on developing 'commitment to learning'. When working with Jackie Beere as part of a QCA research project, an activity was developed which aimed to motivate, develop the 5Rs and make links between subjects for a group of less engaged Year 8 learners. Crucially, it needed to have transferable elements so that other teachers could adapt it to suit their requirements. Learning teams were created with the objective of completing various tasks connected with the Olympic Games. Although the Olympic Games provided the medium, this content could easily be replaced with a more subject-specific content whilst still retaining the features which were shown in lessons to motivate learners.

Learners reacted in a very positive way to the activity. Some of the less engaged boys demonstrated a commitment to the task which was beyond expectations. Over the series of lessons learners were able to identify how the 5R attributes they were developing could be linked to their success in the adult world. This enabled them to access a 'wiifm' (what's in it for me?) factor which, coupled with a competitive and time bound element in class, kept them focused. Encouraging learners to consider the links between the different tasks and the skills developed in other subject areas motivated them as it became clear that by applying these skills they could succeed at tasks which initially seemed challenging because of the unfamiliar context.

The most successful features of the activity which motivated and engaged learners were:

- Grouping learners in carefully selected teams and then placing the responsibility for success on them. This was done by creating the role of 'team captain' which would rotate within the group. The captain had to lead the planning process and decision making, assess progress and liaise with the teacher. The use of captain's armbands as a tangible sign of responsibility encouraged learners who were less comfortable with the role to develop resilience and rise to the challenge of leadership.

- Giving team members a choice of task within the broader activity. Tasks responded to the range of multiple intelligences and learning preferences so learners could opt for a task which suited them. Learners were given the option to design their own task and creative learners liked this flexibility. Names and tasks were logged on the planning sheet. Choosing the task gave learners a sense of ownership, control and the responsibility to complete to a good standard since they had committed to it publicly as part of the planning process.

- Allocating different points to tasks created a competitive element which, combined with a time bound environment, developed an appropriate sense of pressure which many students seemed to thrive on.

- Providing learners with a planning sheet encouraged reflection, enabled assessment for learning against their own success criteria and meant that learners could identify how well the team was progressing. Team members took on the role of 'teacher' and used a range of strategies to support and cajole those who were not seen to be pulling their weight!

- Explicitly discussing with learners when, how and why they might be developing the 5Rs and then linking these attributes to success in the adult world enabled the process to be presented as investing in learners' futures – reinforcing the wiifm dimension.

- Allowing a controlled degree of chaos as learners passed through the 'storming' to 'performing' part of the team-building process meant that (eventually) a calm and purposeful atmosphere was created which the learners were entirely responsible for. This also provided the opportunity to credit those learners who had demonstrated the 5Rs in reaching this point.

- The end product was the result of choices made by the team. This created a sense of pride in their achievements which raised self-esteem which would hopefully benefit other lessons.

As with all teaching and learning methods, this series of lessons would not be appropriate to use all the time. There are trade-offs to be had with time spent focusing on progression through subject attainment levels. However, the reduction in content in the new Key Stage 3 National Curriculum enables subject teachers to make the time to deliver a series of lessons using their subject content but via an activity focused on process and the development of the 5Rs. If engaging with learners in this way raises motivation and self-esteem then it can only be a good thing for their approach to future lessons.

Our challenge now is to support subject teachers in the creation of activities in this style which are clearly linked to their subject content and do not compromise the 'academic' quality of the end product. The reviewing of schemes of work as a result of the new National Curriculum provides an opportunity for teachers to incorporate this style of activity into their schemes. Developing motivation, responsibility and resilience should go a long way towards creating successful learners and confident individuals who can leave the school 'nest' and fly in the outside world.

Catherine Johnson
Cheslyn Hay Sports and Community High School

Case study: Thomas Clarkson Community College, Wisbech

As a Fresh Start school with an Ofsted pending, the challenge to find a short-term solution to re-engaging students (and staff!) was huge at this large rural secondary school. With over 80 of the 230 intake joining Year 7 in 2007 with Level 3 SATs scores one answer was to teach these students in classes studying a competency curriculum with one main teacher. Led by an enthusiastic History teacher and accommodated in a refurbished special set of classrooms, TC3 was created. It delivered literacy and numeracy and topic-based learning based on the three competences, successful learners, confident individuals and responsible citizens, with a progression model taken from *The Learner's Toolkit* (Beere, 2007).

The project was a huge success both in developing the self-confidence of many of the students as well as raising their levels of achievement. Having the same teacher for much of the time gave them stability and consistent messages, and the ethos of TC3 was a school within a school where 'teachers made it easy for us to learn'. Students liked and understood the importance of the competences as they felt they were 'what we need for life'. An interesting observation from the TC3 leader is that the third competence, responsible citizens, became the most important to develop in the students through regular teamwork and a focus on developing empathy and communication skills.

Exclusions for Year 7 dropped and tests demonstrated core skills had improved by the end of the year through the competency approach. Perhaps even more importantly, a new enthusiasm is sweeping the staffroom; the TC3 leader Mark Gore openly admits it has given him 'a new lease' on teaching life as he plans for next year and spreads the word about the impact of his new curriculum.

Impact

The students have made remarkable progress with their academic achievements with 73% on target to achieve their predicted KS3 grade. See the table below for results derived from Year 7 end-of-year tests and teacher assessments. Fischer Family Trust baseline data was used to set targets.

	English	Maths	Science	All core
Above target	28.79%	7.02%	12.50%	16.58%
On target	53.03%	66.67%	50.00%	56.15%
Towards target	18.18%	24.56%	34.38%	25.67%
Under target	0	1.75%	3.13%	1.60%

The Science department have now embraced the competences and are building them into their schemes of work as the project progresses into next year and in the long term the plan is for the school's new Building Schools for the Future design vision to ensure this type of curriculum will be at the heart of the transformation of Thomas Clarkson Community College.

Mark Dove
Thomas Clarkson Community College

Section 2

The Projects

The sample projects provided here attempt to combine crucial subject content in a way that is relevant to students' lives. The projects are designed to engage students in active learning which will develop the skills required by the KS3 curriculum. Each project has the following format: a project scheme of work with the PLTS objectives, followed by lesson materials for the students and separate teacher notes giving a model for delivery. These projects are simply a starting point to help you develop your own projects and link in your own subjects and skills for your competency curriculum. We expect the projects to be amended and developed for each school's context. The only compulsory elements are the first project and the focus on the PLTS competences as part of the assessment model.

Brain Breakthrough

The first project contains crucial content on the brain and how it learns. This work helps students understand more about their brains, the PLTS and why they matter. It is best to complete this project first as it introduces concepts such as emotional intelligence, learning styles and multiple intelligence. These concepts are important to give students a language for learning which they can use throughout their competency course. Developing the PLTS effectively will depend on the students learning about metacognition and how reflection can enhance thinking.

Brain Breakthrough also introduces students to teamwork and how to work effectively together. As many of the following projects will involve working in teams, it is vital to explore what makes a good team member and how students can improve their teamworking skills.

An important part of this project deals with interpersonal skills and how to consciously develop them. There is also an examination of the nature of thinking skills. The final part of this project involves the students exploring an aspect of neuroscience that interests them and sharing it with the whole class.

The project also introduces students to the concept of self-assessment of the PLTS and keeping track of their progress. An essential foundation for a really effective PLTS competency curriculum is for students to be able to take control of their learning and thinking skills

Much of the content of this project would normally be delivered in PSHEE or Learning to Learn lessons. This project can be supplemented with extra lessons from Jackie Beere's *The Learner's Toolkit* as required.

Fair Trade

This project provides an opportunity to consider world trade and how it impacts on all of us. Students use data-handling skills to analyse a government's spending plans and have the chance to create their own fair trade product and sell it. They will investigate worldwide trade and the ethical elements of globalisation, including presenting their research findings to each other. This project has many subject links and many opportunities to develop the PLTS in the group activities. Learning is demonstrated through presentations and assessment of progress against the PLTS in the Tracker Pack.

Money, Money, Money

This project addresses the challenging issues of managing money and the concepts of wealth and materialism. Students have to investigate how to design budgets for various projects such as refurbishing their classroom. It also includes a self-assessment tool to help students understand how they act as spenders and a design element in which they consider how to create and design their own currency. The project includes a Community of Enquiry activity where the students undertake controlled philosophical discussion group work, examining whether being rich makes you happy. Abstract thinking skills are developed here as well as speaking and listening competences.

There are clear links to functional numeracy and PSHEE in this project and there is also a link to a Bible story which considers our own personal relationship with money. The usual elements of teamwork and communication skills are developed through the activities and there is an opportunity to link the content with the historical impact of the 2008-9 'credit crunch'.

Saving Planet Earth

This project develops independent research skills and is related to the environmental issues of real concern to students in the twenty-first century. Following the reading of a short story which engages thinking about how man impacts on the planet, students can relate this topic to their own lives. The project begins with areas for teamwork and research and goes on to develop opportunities for creative thinking in which students create drama, art or music productions to represent their ideas.

In addition, the students have to apply their thinking skills to design eco-friendly homes or re-cycling projects as part of their teamwork activities. There are many links from this project to the Science and Geography curriculum as well as English and ICT assessment opportunities.

Project 1: Brain Breakthrough – Your Learning, It's Personal!

Activity No.	Teaching and Learning Overview	PLTS Competence Objectives	Outcomes	Further Subject Opportunities
1 **Estimated time** **1 hour**	**It's the brain buster!** Students will investigate the concept of competency-based learning and be introduced to the PLTS. They will explore the key competencies and how to track their progress using the Tracker Pack. Students will engage with target-setting for personal aspirations and goals. Students will develop their peer-assessment techniques using praise and advice. PLTS focus: P and L	■ To cooperate with others either one-to-one or in a team. ■ To set yourself targets and work towards them. ■ To understand the power and flexibility of the brain and how it can be developed using the competences.	■ Students will complete a goal-setting worksheet. ■ Students should record where they are currently working in their Tracker Pack. ■ Students will know what is meant by the term PLTS.	Learning to Learn (L2L) Study Skills Careers and Work Related Learning Science
2 **Estimated time** **2 hours**	**Where are you going?** Students will be engaging in the goal-setting worksheet to help them develop goal- and target-setting skills. Students will consider: Famous personalities and what attitudes they have alongside their talent that has helped them become successful. PLTS focus: P and L	■ To cooperate with others either one-to-one or in a team. ■ To cooperate with others acting as a team leader or a team member. ■ To develop your ability to manage disappointment and celebrate success. ■ To increase your ability to think logically and plan targets for yourself.	■ Students will set themselves personal goals for their future success. ■ Students will consider the success of famous personalities (like Lewis Hamilton) and consider what makes them successful beyond their raw talent. ■ Students will record their personal goals in their Tracker Packs.	L2L Study Skills Careers and Work Related Learning English/Literacy Citizenship

Activity No.	Teaching and Learning Overview	PLTS Competence Objectives	Outcomes	Further Subject Opportunities
3 **Estimated time 1 hour**	**Make the team** Students will consider the term *democracy* and explore methods to help govern their competency lessons. Students will develop their literacy skills and knowledge of key words like *anarchy*, *democracy* and *ballot*. Students will develop their speech-writing skills and be able to give reasons for their points of view. Students will develop their speaking and listening skills by presenting manifesto speeches to the rest of the class. Students will vote for the best class manifesto and display it in their classroom. There is the optional use of Philosophy for Children (P4C) methods for this lesson—for more details about P4C visit http://www.sapere.org.uk PLTS focus: P and L	■ To develop empathy with other people's values and feelings. ■ To cooperate with others acting as a team leader or a team member. ■ To actively contribute to the class and have a say in how your classroom functions. ■ To increase your literacy skills and develop your speaking and listening.	■ Students will create a class manifesto speech stating what they consider to be essential for the best learning environment. They will be encouraged to justify their points. ■ Students will present their speeches to the rest of the class. ■ Students will take part in a secret ballot to vote for their class manifesto. Students may take part in a Philosophy for Children Community of Enquiry focusing on democracy and rules.	L2L Study Skills Careers and Work Related learning English/Literacy Citizenship
4 **Estimated time 2 hours**	**Building brilliant communication skills** Students will learn about the importance of body language and non-verbal communication for creating effective rapport with others.	■ To cooperate with others either one-to-one or in a team. ■ To develop awareness of yourself as a learner. ■ To effectively participate in small group work.	■ Students will present their role-plays about good and bad listening styles. ■ Students will be able to describe what excellent listening looks like. ■ Students will create a list of top tips for excellent listening.	All curriculum areas Literacy

	Activity	Objectives	Outcomes	Curriculum
	Students will consider what makes good listening and work in pairs or small groups to demonstrate good and poor listening. Students will store their top tips for excellent listening in their Tracker Packs. PLTS focus: P and L			All curriculum areas
5 **Estimated time** **1 hour**	**Teamwork – Together Everyone Achieves More** Students will work as part of a team and identify the different roles that make teams work successfully. Students will have the opportunity to work as a team imagining they are creating their own country. Students will store their top tips for teamwork in their Tracker Packs. PLTS focus: P, L and T	■ To cooperate with others acting as a team leader or a team member. ■ To develop awareness of yourself as a learner. ■ To develop your ability to compromise with others. ■ To develop your creative thinking and back up your ideas with arguments.	■ Students will be able to describe the different roles that make up a successful team. ■ Students will create a list of top tips for excellent teamwork. ■ Students will work as part of a team to create their own country. ■ Students will present their ideas to the rest of the class. ■ Students will practise giving each other praise and advice.	All curriculum areas
6 **Estimated time** **1 hour**	**Picture this – Making learning maps** Students will create their own learning maps. Teachers can decide what the focus of the learning map should be, e.g. your favourite subject. Students will store their completed learning map in their Tracker Pack. PLTS focus: L and T	■ To develop awareness of yourself as a learner. ■ To develop your creative thinking skills.	■ Students will create a learning map and store in their Tracker Packs.	All curriculum areas

Activity No.	Teaching and Learning Overview	PLTS Competence Objectives	Outcomes	Further Subject Opportunities
7 **Estimated time** **1 hour**	**Multiple intelligences** Students will increase their knowledge about the different ways there are to be smart. Students will rate themselves against the multiple intelligences. Students will record their strengths and weaknesses in their Tracker Pack with targets for developing their weaker multiple intelligences. PLTS focus: L	■ To develop your ability to self-assess your strengths and weaknesses. ■ To set yourself goals and targets and work towards them. ■ To understand the power and flexibility of the brain and how it can be developed using the competences.	■ Students will complete Smarts worksheets and give reasons for their decisions.	All curriculum areas
8 **Estimated time** **1 hour**	**Emotional intelligence (1)** Students will consider how they can control their moods. They will consider the importance of body language and how this can influence moods. Students will create mood monitors that they can use at home or in school. Students will store a copy of their mood timeline in their Tracker Pack. PLTS focus: P and L	■ To develop your ability to manage disappointment and celebrate success. ■ To develop empathy with other people's values and feelings. ■ To increase your ability to think logically and plan targets for yourself.	■ Students will create a mood monitor for their personal use. ■ Students will complete a mood timeline and store in their Tracker Pack.	All curriculum areas

9 **Estimated time** **2 hours**	**Emotional intelligence (2)** Students will discover what the term *self-belief* means and how to develop an optimistic approach to life and learning. Students will use their imagination to predict their futures and create superheroes and positive, emotionally intelligent slogans that they can use to help them maintain optimistic and positive attitudes. PLTS focus: P and T	■ To develop your ability to cope with challenges more confidently. ■ To develop your ability to be optimistic in your approach to learning. ■ To develop your ability to participate with others effectively.	■ Students will be able to explain the terms *self-belief* and *optimism*. ■ Students will create a positive, emotionally intelligent slogan for themselves. ■ Students will create a superhero that will demonstrate positive moods and self-belief.	L2L Study Skills PSHE ICT English/Literacy History
10 **Estimated time** **1 hour**	**What sort of thinker are you?** Students will consider the two sides of the brain and investigate how to grow their whole brain and develop their metacognition skills. PLTS focus: T, P and L	■ To increase your ability to make changes in lots of differing ways. ■ To set yourself targets and work towards them. ■ To understand the power and flexibility of the brain and how it can be developed using the competences. ■ To develop your ability to think in creative ways.	■ Students will be able to describe logical and creative sides and traits of the brain. ■ Students will be able to describe ways they can grow their whole brains. ■ Students will record the targets they have set themselves to grow their whole brain in their Tracker Packs.	L2L Study Skills

Activity No.	Teaching and Learning Overview	PLTS Competence Objectives	Outcomes	Further Subject Opportunities
11 **Estimated time 5 hours**	**Putting your PLTS into practice** Students will undertake a research assignment to investigate a learning style. Students will present their findings back to the class. Students may work individually, in pairs or in teams—how they are grouped is at the teacher's discretion. Students will use peer-assessment techniques using praise and advice. Students will work in teams to complete a piece of display work entitled 'Our Learning Tree'. Using one piece of large coloured paper students will work as a team to draw around their hands and cut them out (keeping wastage to a minimum) to create 'leaves'—these can be illustrated with key words, pictures, ideas and anything they have learnt in project Brain Breakthrough. Students will complete a self-review of their progress in project Brain Breakthrough and record the details in their Tracker packs. PLTS focus: L, P and T	■ To cooperate with others either one-to-one or in a team. ■ To cooperate with others acting as a team leader or a team member. ■ To increase your ability to think logically and plan targets for yourself. ■ To develop your ability to think creatively. ■ To increase your ability to work independently of the teacher.	■ Students will be able to describe what the terms *visual*, *auditory* and *kinaesthetic* mean and how people learn differently. ■ Students will be able to describe what each team role entails and how it contributes to team success. ■ Students will create a PowerPoint presentation about their learning style using animation effectively. ■ Students will develop their communication skills by presenting their work to the rest of the class. ■ Students will develop their peer-assessment techniques using praise and advice methods. ■ Students will complete a self-review of their progress in the project and store in their Tracker Packs.	L2L Study Skills English/Literacy ICT

Curriculum links

These links are edited from the relevant subject links at:

http://curriculum.qca.org.uk/key-stages-3-and-4/index.aspx. The following are taken from the PSHE Personal Wellbeing recommended programme of study.

PSHE Personal Wellbeing

Pupils need to understand a range of key concepts in order to deepen and broaden their knowledge, skills and understanding of personal wellbeing.

These include: personal identities (understanding that identity is affected by a range of factors, including a positive sense of self; recognising that the way in which personal qualities, attitudes, skills and achievements are evaluated affects confidence and self-esteem; understanding that self-esteem can change with personal circumstances); healthy lifestyles (recognising that healthy lifestyles, and the wellbeing of self and others, depend on information and making responsible choices; understanding that physical, mental, sexual and emotional health affect our ability to lead fulfilling lives, and that there is help and support available when they are threatened; dealing with growth and change as normal parts of growing up); risk (understanding risk in both positive and negative terms and understanding that individuals need to manage risk to themselves and others in a range of situations; appreciating that pressure can be used positively or negatively to influence others in situations involving risk; developing the confidence to try new ideas and face challenges safely, individually and in groups); and relationships (understanding that relationships affect everything we do in our lives and that relationship skills have to be learnt and practised; understanding that people have multiple roles and responsibilities in society and that making positive relationships and contributing to groups, teams and communities is important; understanding that relationships can cause strong feelings and emotions).

Pupils need to make progress with essential skills and key processes relating to critical reflection: being able to reflect critically on their own and others' values; reflect on personal strengths, achievements and areas for development; recognise how others see them and give and receive feedback; identify and use strategies for setting and meeting personal targets in order to increase motivation; reflect on feelings and identify positive ways of understanding, managing and expressing strong emotions and challenging behaviour; and develop self-awareness by reflecting critically on their behaviour and its impact on others.

In terms of decision making and managing risk, pupils should be able to: use knowledge and understanding to make informed choices about safety, health and wellbeing; use strategies for resisting unhelpful peer influence and pressure; know when and how to get help; identify how managing feelings and emotions effectively supports decision making and risk management.

When developing relationships and working with others pupils should be able to: use social skills to build and maintain a range of positive relationships; use the social skill of negotiation within relationships, recognise their rights and responsibilities and that their actions have consequences; use the social skills of communication, negotiation, assertiveness and collaboration; value differences between people and demonstrate empathy and a willingness to learn about people different from themselves. Study should include examples of diverse values encountered in society and the clarification of personal values, and the knowledge and skills needed for setting realistic targets and personal goals.

Teacher's notes: It's the brain buster!

Resources: Lined/plain paper, copy of Tracker Pack for each student, copy of PLTS for all students, option to use a visual aid model of a human brain.

PLTS objective

By the end of this lesson students will be able to describe the PLTS competences. Students will be able to make connections between the competences and skills they will need in life to be successful. They will understand the power and flexibility of the brain and how it can be developed using the competences (L and P).

Get excited!

Teacher poses big questions about the brain for class discussion.

Main learning activities

Teacher-led explanation of what competency learning is using the Tracker Pack sheet to introduce students to the PLTS competences and the Tracker Pack.

Students then complete a worksheet considering what competences they have begun to develop already and those they will find harder to progress.

Make clear to students that competences are not something you can quickly achieve—you work on them all your life. Competency learning is lifelong learning!

Encourage students to make connections beyond school of how competencies will help in all areas of their lives.

How did I do?

Students should record where they are in their Tracker Pack.

Subject links

Learning to Learn (L2L)
Study Skills
Careers and Work Related Learning
Science

iT'S THE BRAIN BUSTER!

PLTS objective: To understand the power and flexibility of the brain and how it can be developed using the competences.

GET EXCITED!

Consider this headline: 'Scientists discover that the brain has amazing undiscovered powers'. What could they be?

FACTS

Your brain has 100 billion neurons (brain cells).

You learn by making connections between neurons.

Your brain is more powerful than a computer the size of Wembley Stadium.

MAIN ACTIVITY

What undiscovered powers could your brain have?

What brain power would help you with learning?

Growing your competences (a cluster of skills and abilities) will help you be a successful learner. What skills and abilities would you like to develop to make you a great learner?

Competence	Impact	Saying
Self-discipline Listening Optimism	Get things done	No pain, no gain

Look at the PLTS and decide how good you are at each of these.

Think of a famous person that might be a top scorer for each of the PLTS.

Create a PLTS card for your bedside table. Use the sayings and create cartoon pictures to help you remember the PLTS.

Teacher's notes: Where are you going?

Resources: Lined/plain paper.

PLTS objective

Students will be able to set goals and think ahead.

Get excited!

Pose the question: 'What would you do if you won £100,000?' and spend one minute discussing it. Then take one minute thinking about and discussing student's future dream jobs. What would they do if they knew they could not fail?

Main learning activities

Complete a worksheet thinking about famous successful people and setting personal goals.

Students then imagine themselves in the future and have to describe their amazing success stories and interview each other.

Teachers need to encourage debate about successful personalities and that behind their success is not just talent but a real passion for fulfilling their goals.

Use contemporary examples like racing driver Lewis Hamilton etc.

How did I do?

Encourage students to create a newspaper headline they can share with the rest of the class that reflects their amazing future achievements.

Students should discuss how the competences will help them achieve their goals and record their goals in their Tracker Pack.

Subject links

Learning to Learn
Study Skills
Careers and Work Related Learning
English/Literacy
Citizenship

WHERE ARE YOU GOING?

PLTS objective: Being able to set goals and think ahead.

GET EXCITED!

What would you do if you won £100,000 pounds? What is your dream job of the future? Just imagining this sparks off neurons because having a dream or goal produces the chemicals that drive you to succeed.

MAIN ACTIVITY

'Where are you going?' said the rabbit to Alice. 'I don't know,' said Alice.

'Well, you will never get there then,' sneered the rabbit.

 Create a story about a successful footballer or pop star. Imagine you know how they got where they are today. Write the story of their lives in a paragraph. Share your stories. As well as their skills, what themes did all your stories have in common?

....

....

....

....

Most successful people had goals and dreams long before they make it big. How did they do it?

1. They had a goal.

2. They believed they could achieve it.

3. They used strategies that worked to achieve their goals.

PROJECT 1 - BRAIN BREAKTHROUGH
WHERE ARE YOU GOING?
- CONTINUED

PLTS objective: Being able to set goals and think ahead.

If *they* can do it, *you* can do it ... but first you have to set yourself short-term and long-term goals and think about how you will set about achieving them.

My long-term goal/dream is ....

....

I will achieve this by ....

....

Today I will ....

....

The time to start working towards your goals is *now*. Simply by writing down and committing to a goal you make a new and important connection in the brain. A part of the brain lights up whenever a challenge or goal is created.

Create three important goals for this year:

1. ....

....

2. ....

....

3. ....

....

PROJECT 1 - BRAIN BREAKTHROUGH
WHERE ARE YOU GOING? - CONTINUED

PLTS objective: Being able to set goals and think ahead.

Create two personal goals for the next five years:

1. ....

....

2. ....

....

It is five years from now. Describe a day in your life in the present tense.

Task: Interview your partner as a 30-year-old, talking about their school life and how they achieved their amazing success.

Extension task: At home, research into the lives of your heroes and how they achieved success.

HOW DID I DO?

How can the competencies help you achieve your goals? Write a headline in a local newspaper about your amazing achievements.

....

....

....

....

Teacher's notes: Make the team

ACTIVITY 3 · PROJECT 1 · 1 HOUR

Resources: Lined/plain paper, optional use of ICT.

PLTS objective

By the end of this lesson students will be able to explain the key tips for successful teamwork.

Get excited!

How do you learn best? Students can verbally contribute their suggestions for how we learn best and these can be displayed for everyone to see.

Main learning activities

Teacher-led explanation of *democracy*. Students to consider all the things they have ever voted for and share with each other, for example, *Pop Idol*, form reps, etc.

Students will work in teams and create a set of rules for an effective learning environment.

Students' manifesto speeches should reflect their ideas and be presented to the rest of the class.

How did I do?

Students should be asked how they think they worked in a team and analyse what worked well and what didn't. The teacher needs to allow students to analyse what makes teams work well.

Students should vote for the best set of classroom rules.

Students should record their golden team player targets in their Tracker Packs.

Subject links

Learning to Learn
Study Skills
Careers and Work Related Learning
Literacy
English
Citizenship

MAKE THE TEAM

PLTS objective: Developing teamwork skills.

GET EXCITED!

How do you learn best? Munching? Drinking? Sitting up? Lying down? With friends? With music on? We all have different needs, so how can we make your classroom good for you?

MAIN ACTIVITY

PLTS lessons are about teamwork and independent learning but how can we make sure the learning environment is good for everyone? Take a vote on it! If we all agree and understand the rules then we all feel safe and happy. This is the democratic approach.

Democratic values are important for your learning environment. What does democracy mean? Think of three words that sum up democracy for you.

1. ....

2. ....

3. ....

Make a list of everything you have ever voted for—from television shows to school elections.

....

....

....

....

....

Values for life include love, loyalty, friendship, money, fun … What are your top three values?

1. ....

2. ....

3. ....

You vote according to your values. Values are what you believe to be important in life. They help you make good rules.

MAKE THE TEAM - CONTINUED

PLTS objective: Developing teamwork skills.

Now make a set of five rules for your teamwork activities. Get into teams of five. Now look at each others' rules. Vote on your favourite rules for the team. What should be the five rules for your teamwork?

1. ....

2. ....

3. ....

4. ....

5. ....

Now prepare a manifesto for your team. This should include:

- Team name ....

- Team shield with visual representations of each rule.

PROJECT 1 - BRAIN BREAKTHROUGH
MAKE THE TEAM - CONTINUED

PLTS objective: Developing teamwork skills.

• Five team rules and why you have chosen them (this may be linked to your values).

1. ....

2. ....

3. ....

4. ....

5. ....

• A speech you can deliver to the class that explains all about your team.

....

....

....

....

....

....

....

....

....

HOW DID I DO?

How did you work as a team?

....

Who had the best set of rules?

....

....

Teacher's notes: Building brilliant communication skills

Resources: Lined/plain paper, optional use of ICT/video cameras/digital cameras.

PLTS objective

By the end of these lessons you will be able to communicate successfully, relating well with others in a team or on a one-to-one basis.

Get excited!

Allow five minutes to listen to the sounds around and within the room, discuss the body language that is present and decide what it might reflect people are saying.

The teacher could alternatively demonstrate or ask students to 'act' out different examples of body language for the rest of the class to guess. The teacher should aim to get students to understand that non-verbal communication is just as important as verbal communication.

Main learning activities

Students should work with a partner or in a small group to develop their different listening skills and strategies. Students should be encouraged to take part in a role-play of their own creation to demonstrate positive and negative body language and how this shows good or poor listening.

Students could have the option of recording their ideas using video cameras/digital cameras if appropriate.

How did I do?

Students should be able to describe and demonstrate what excellent listening looks like and how it is a skill that will bring them rapport and success in life.

Students should record their golden listening targets in their Tracker Packs.

Subject links

Across the whole curriculum

BUILDING BRILLIANT COMMUNICATION SKILLS

PLTS objective: To become a great communicator so that you work well with others.

GET EXCITED!

Listen to the sounds around you now – jot down everything you can hear. Now listen to your insides—what can you hear? Listening also requires you to look at *body language* to understand what someone is really saying. Look around the room and see what bodies are saying to you. Are they happy, focused or fidgety?

MAIN ACTIVITY

Some people learn well when they are listening. This is a very important skill to acquire as so much of what we have to learn requires *good listening skills*.

How do you know you have heard something? What mental processes go on after you have heard something important?

1. In pairs, find out how good you are at listening. Here are some activities that will involve careful listening: Tell your partner some details of your last holiday—make them repeat back to you the main points.

2. Now tell each other a story about what you did last weekend—without words, just actions.

3. Show the following emotions through your facial expressions: happiness, anger, sadness, not understanding, curiosity.

If you can learn to read body language then you will start to gain *rapport*, which is a French word for brilliant communication. To get good rapport you need good eye contact, a slight head tilt and to mirror and match the person you are listening to. Try not to block by folding your arms, look away or stare too much, or turn your body away.

TASK 1

(In threes with one observer) imagine you are at a counselling session. One of you is the counsellor, one the client. Tell the counsellor your real (or imaginary) problems about school or home in three or four minutes. The counsellor then has to repeat back to you a summary of the problems and suggest some solutions. The observer reports back on how good the listening was.

Now swap and this time the listener has to use body language to encourage the client. The observer can now report on the listening and the body language and demonstrate the best to the class.

BUILDiNG BRiLLiANT COMMUNiCATiON SKiLLS – CONTiNUED

PLTS objective: To become a great communicator so that you work well with others.

TASK 2

Try listening to your internal dialogue—the voice that talks to you inside your head. It often gives you a running commentary on what you are doing and what you are going to do. What sort of voice is it? Is it your voice? Try to make it positive and encouraging. This can be very motivating.

Look at this example: You are asked to do a bungee jump for charity. There are two thoughts that may come into your head. Your negative voice says, 'I might die! People get injured. I might chicken out at the last minute and look like a fool.' Your positive voice says, 'That could be exciting. I can do it and think how good it would make me feel. I will be making money for someone else.' Which one would you think?

Practice now making your internal voice say something positive to you. Make the most of self-talk to build your confidence and self-belief.

AVOID – Negative self-talk	**INCREASE – Positive self-talk**
I can't do it	I'm brilliant and beautiful!
She hates me	I can do anything if I work hard enough
I've never been good at exams	I love exams
My writing is rubbish	I am an excellent friend
No one likes me	I am very determined to get it right
It's bound to go wrong	I am born lucky
Add some more …	*Add some more …*
....	....
....	....
....	....
....	....
....	....

Mind–body connection. Say each of the positive statements above and practice putting the body language with it—it's much more powerful.

BUILDING BRILLIANT COMMUNICATION SKILLS - CONTINUED

ACTIVITY 4

PROJECT 1 PAGE 3

PLTS objective: To become a great communicator so that you work well with others.

TASK 3

Stand back-to-back with a partner and show the two voices—positive and negative—as you are asked these questions by a third person: Do you want to come to my party? Have you done your homework? Can you wash the dishes, please? Do you fancy me?

Tips for great communication:

- Listen with your ears and your body.
- Smile and nod.
- Tune in to any feedback your audience is giving you.
- Be present—don't think of other things.
- Keep good eye contact.
- Be enthusiastic and excited about what you are saying.
- Be clear and precise.
- Use gestures to help you.

HOW DID I DO?

Finish these sentences:

A good listener always...

I can get good rapport by..

Teacher's notes: Teamwork – Together Everyone Achieves More

Resources: Lined/plain paper, large format sugar paper, coloured pens, pictures of successful teams (optional).

PLTS objective

By the end of this lesson you will be able to successfully act as a team leader or team member.

Get excited!

Think of the best teams you know—why do they succeed? Allow one minute to discuss in pairs and then a maximum of four minutes to feedback to the whole class.

If possible the teacher could have collected pictures from newspapers/magazines and compiled them into a presentation to help stimulate this discussion about successful teams.

Main learning activities

Teamwork and being a successful team member is a skill that can be learnt and practised. Lessons can provide lots of opportunities to practise this skill. Forming teams and identifying what team members need to do to make their team successful is key to this lesson.

Spend time discussing as a whole class the team roles and what they mean. The teacher should support each team to make sure everyone is fulfilling his or her team role.

Allow the students time to practise these skills by getting them to work in teams to 'create their own country'.

How did I do?

Students should be encouraged to review their teamwork, how well they performed their roles and what they can learn from this experience of teamwork.

Students should record their golden team player targets in their Tracker Packs.

Subject links

Across the whole curriculum

TEAMWORK - TOGETHER EVERYONE ACHIEVES MORE

PLTS objective: To practise working together in a team and taking on various roles.

GET EXCITED!

Think of the best teams you know. Why do they succeed?

MAIN ACTIVITY

Form your team, allocate the following roles and make a note of them:

- *Team leader* – leads the whole team and makes the final decisions for the group, often presenting ideas back to the class.
- *Timekeeper* – reminds the team how much time they have left and makes sure all the jobs get done.
- *Notetaker* – keeps notes of all information and decisions.
- *Includer* – makes sure everyone has a chance to speak and have their opinions heard.
- *Listener* – makes sure everyone in the team is listening to each other and also not making too much noise and disturbing other groups.

TASK

As a team your task is to create your own country. You have some paper and pens and one hour to create a national identity for your country. You will need to present your country to the whole class.

HOW DID I DO?

Rate yourself out of ten as a member of the group.

....

Rate each other out of ten in their roles.

....

Share your scores and discuss how you can improve.

Teacher's notes: Picture this – Making learning maps

ACTIVITY 6 PROJECT 1 1 HOUR

Resources: Lined/plain paper, coloured pens.

PLTS objective

By the end of this lesson students will know how to create learning maps and how this can help them become golden learners by developing their self-awareness and creativity as a learner.

Get excited!

Imagine a frog! This is a teacher-led visualisation to aid students' understanding of how internally visualising information can help learning.

Main learning activities

Create a learning map of yourself as a learner.

The lesson suggestion is to create a learning map about your favourite subject. The teacher may select an alternative focus for the class/student learning map if appropriate.

Creating learning maps is a skill that becomes more polished and accomplished over time. Students should not worry at this stage about its overall presentation— it's about getting down as much as they can, including pictures, symbols, colour, etc.

How did I do?

Students should keep a copy of the learning map they create in their Tracker Pack.

Subject links

Across the whole curriculum

PROJECT 1 – BRAIN BREAKTHROUGH
PiCTURE THiS –
MAKiNG LEARNiNG MAPS

ACTIVITY 6
PROJECT 1   1 HOUR

PLTS objective: To develop your self-awareness and creativity as a learner.

GET EXCiTED!

Use your eyes to see and use your brain to create visual pictures. Imagine a frog sitting on your table. What colour is it? Touch it and feel its slimy skin. Now try a cat—hear it purring. If you find it hard to visualise these animals, it could be hard for you to use internal visualising for learning so you need to practise!

Here are two powerful learning tools to help you make the most of your visual learning.

MAiN ACTiViTY

Creating a learning map involves using all the important information you need to know but writing it down in a way that is brain-friendly and captures your visual imagination. Most of the time we write our notes in lists and paragraphs. This does not always help us remember them.

Good learning maps use colour, images, symbols and words. These are all brain-friendly and give us visual stimulation. They start with a central idea and grow branches in all directions as ideas flow. It doesn't matter if they are not artistic or organised.

Take your favourite subject and try to create a learning map of everything you know about it. Put the main themes on the trunk and branches and all the other ideas on the little twigs that come from them. It doesn't matter if it is untidy or not logical as long as you understand it—just get as much down as you can. Now add lots of pictures and symbols to make it more interesting and memorable.

Give it to a neighbour to study for five minutes—then test how much they have learnt about that subject. Ask them how they remembered bits of the map. Was it through the pictures or the words? Did they see the map inside their heads? If they did they were using their visual memory.

Now try creating a learning map for another subject you find more difficult or for a book you are studying—don't forget to use lots of colour and pictures.

Teacher's notes: Multiple intelligences – There are lots of ways to be clever!

Resources: Lined/plain paper, Post-it notes, copy of the Smarts worksheet for each student.

PLTS objective

By the end of this lesson students will have a deeper self-awareness of themselves as learners and gained a greater vocabulary for describing themselves as learners.

Get excited!

Encourage students to think about the different ways in which they are clever and how they have different talents—encourage them to think beyond subjects at school. Students may prefer to write down their ideas on Post-it notes and bring them to the board at the front rather than share out loud. The teacher can then select different examples to talk about.

Main learning activities

Students should complete the worksheet about the different Smarts, rating themselves and explaining their decisions.

Students can put their teamwork skills into practice again whilst planning a school visit that would encourage use of *all* the intelligences. They could then present their ideas to the rest of the group for praise and advice.

How did I do?

Students should record in their Tracker Packs their two best Smarts strengths and alongside this set two targets for improving their weaker Smarts.

Subject links

Across the whole curriculum
Learning to Learn
Study Skills

PROJECT 1 - BRAIN BREAKTHROUGH
MULTIPLE INTELLIGENCES - THERE ARE LOTS OF WAYS TO BE CLEVER!

PLTS objective: Develop self-awareness about how learning works for you.

GET EXCITED!

TASK 1: HOW MANY WAYS AM I CLEVER?

Find out in this section how you are intelligent in many different ways and how you can use this to improve your learning.

Write a list of three things you are good at and say why. Is it the same to be clever at playing football and clever at Maths? Are you clever if you can make plants grow or draw fantastic pictures? Discuss what it means to be clever.

Neuroscientists now think that intelligence isn't just being good at Maths or English but there are many different ways to be intelligent. You have *multiple intelligences*. There are lots of ways you are smart—here are some of them:

- Interpersonal – people smart
- Logical – number smart
- Artisitc – picture smart
- Musical – music smart

- Intrapersonal – self smart
- Linguistic – word smart
- Kinesthetic/physical – body smart
- Naturalist – nature smart

Discuss each one with a friend and then fill in the box to rate yourself on each of the Smarts.

People smart

Are you good at getting on with people—not just your friends but adults, children, teachers? Are you a good listener, showing consideration and tolerance?

How do I rate myself?

*1 (rubbish)*_____*10 (brilliant)*

Explain how/why you decided:

Self smart

Understanding yourself and the way you work is vital for success in life. Can you control your moods and motivate yourself? Can you explain the way you behave in certain situations? Are you good at setting yourself targets and sticking to promises?

How do I rate myself?

*1 (rubbish)*_____*10 (brilliant)*

Explain how/why you decided:

PLTS objective: Develop self-awareness about how learning works for you.

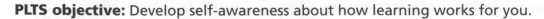

Word smart

If you enjoy reading and talking using a well-developed vocabulary you will be word smart. You may be good at writing essays and stories and enjoy playing around with words and meanings. Your favourite lesson may be English if you are word smart.

How do I rate myself?

1 (rubbish)_____10 (brilliant)

Explain how/why you decided:

Number smart

Are you good at solving problems and sorting things out in a step-by-step fashion? Do you make lists of things to do and work through them? Your favourite subjects may be Maths and Science and you enjoy brainteasers and puzzles. If this sounds like you, you are number smart.

How do I rate myself?

1 (rubbish)_____10 (brilliant)

Explain how/why you decided:

Picture smart

Do you think in pictures? If you enjoy drawing, painting and looking at pictures, these are signs of visual/spatial intelligence. Learning more effectively from maps, graphs and pictures is easy for picture smart people.

How do I rate myself?

1 (rubbish)_____10 (brilliant)

Explain how/why you decided:

Body smart

This is the ability to use your body skilfully in sport, dance or in building and constructing things. If you are strong in this intelligence you will enjoy lessons like PE, Drama and Technology. You will enjoy doing things yourself rather than watching others and sometimes find it hard to sit still!

How do I rate myself?

1 (rubbish)_____10 (brilliant)

Explain how/why you decided:

MULTIPLE INTELLIGENCES - THERE ARE LOTS OF WAYS TO BE CLEVER! - CONTINUED

ACTIVITY 7

PROJECT 1 PAGE 3

PLTS objective: Develop self-awareness about how learning works for you.

Music smart

If you have got good rhythm and enjoy singing or playing an instrument you are likely to have a strong musical intelligence. Do you listen to a variety of music because you want to and can you pick out patterns and instruments that others don't seem to notice? This is another sign of being music smart.

How do I rate myself?

*1 (rubbish)*_____*10 (brilliant)*

Explain how/why you decided:

Nature smart

If you are nature smart then you are aware and interested in plants and animals, and the environment. You may love being outdoors and care about the environment around you. You may be very aware of animal rights issues and hope to have a career in an outdoor environment.

How do I rate myself?

*1 (rubbish)*_____*10 (brilliant)*

Explain how/why you decided:

TASK 2

Think of a time when you used each intelligence. Do you use some more than others? Write down which you have used and when.

HOW DID I DO?

In groups create a school visit that uses *all* the intelligences. Write your schedule for the day.

Teacher's notes: Emotional intelligence (1) – Take control of your moods!

Resources: Lined/plain paper, worksheets for all students, card, paper clips, coloured pens.

PLTS objective

By the end of this lesson you will understand what is meant by emotional intelligence.

Students will take control of their thinking to create positive outcomes.

Get excited!

Students review their current mood state using the worksheet and discuss with a partner why they feel like this.

Main learning activities

Teacher-led explanation about how we choose our moods and how this can affect the outcome of events.

Students complete the worksheet considering what puts them in good and bad moods and how this is reflected in their body language.

Using a piece of card and paper clips students should to create a mood monitor for their personal use in their learning in school and at home.

How did I do?

Students should write down who decides what mood they are in.

Students should complete the mood timcline in their Tracker Pack.

Subject links

Across the whole curriculum
Learning to Learn
Study Skills

EMOTIONAL INTELLIGENCE (1) - TAKE CONTROL OF YOUR MOODS!

PLTS objective: To take control of your thinking and create positive outcomes.

GET EXCITED!

What mood are you in? What puts you in a good/bad mood? Circle on this scale where you think you are:

Despairing … depressed … a bit down … OK … quite good … good … very good … ecstatic

Explain to your neighbour how you know and why you feel like this.

MAIN ACTIVITY

The mood you are in can change the outcome of events—if you can control your moods then you can control your life. What puts you in a bad mood or a good mood? Make a list with two columns.

Your facial expression and your posture are very influenced by your mood. How can you tell what mood someone is in? Fill in this chart to show how body language is affected by mood.

Mood	Signs
Happy	Smiling, sitting up, active, alert
Angry	....
Sad	....
Anxious	....
_____	....
_____	....
_____	....
_____	....
_____	....
_____	....
_____	....

PLTS objective: To take control of your thinking and create positive outcomes.

Mind–body connection

Laugh loudly *now*—just by physically laughing endorphins are triggered that make you feel good.

It is impossible to be in a bad mood if you hold your head up, put your shoulders back and walk with a bounce in your step—try it!

TASK

It is Monday morning breakfast time. Act out the typical scene. Then change the mood of each of the actors to see how it changes the scene.

Your mood has the power to influence others—bad moods are contagious, good moods are infectious and spread happiness.

Create a mood monitor for your bedroom—use card to cut out and make the mood monitor. Write on the different moods and use a paper clip to show your current mood. When you have completed this and shown your own mood, work in pairs to try to change each others' mood.

PLTS objective: To take control of your thinking and create positive outcomes.

How can we change our own mood? Write down three ways:

1. ....

2. ....

3. ....

How can we change each other's moods? Write down three ways:

1. ....

2. ....

3. ....

HOW DID i DO?

Who decides what mood you are in?

....

Teacher's notes: Emotional intelligence (2) – Self-belief and sowing seeds of optimism

Resources: Lined/plain paper.

PLTS objective

By the end of this lesson students will develop their ability to cope more confidently with challenges.

Get excited!

Seat students according to their zodiac star signs and ask each group to state one or two things they might know about their star sign.

Main learning activities

Using the horoscopes from the worksheets the first example is going to make the students wary, sad, suspicious and full of self-doubt.

The second example should affect student's behaviour differently and they think and feel that everyone appreciates them—sowing seeds of optimism.

Students will complete the rest of the worksheet and write a typical horoscope for themselves for this week. They will draw a timeline of their life from their birth until now including the main events and then carry it on until 2050 and put in expected events.

Creating positive slogans and superhero figures will help them maintain positive moods and self-belief in the future.

How did I do?

Students should be able to explain what we mean by the term *self-belief*.

Students should complete the personal thought section in their Tracker Packs.

Subject links

Learning to Learn
Study Skills
PSHE
ICT
English/Literacy
History

EMOTIONAL INTELLIGENCE (2) - SELF-BELIEF AND SOWING SEEDS OF OPTIMISM

PLTS objective: Develop a confident approach to challenges.

GET EXCITED!

Consider: if you think you can or if you think you can't, you are right. Believe in yourself and your skills and abilities. You can be your own worst enemy if you don't believe in yourself. What happens to people who don't believe in themselves?

MAIN ACTIVITY

Think about how we try to predict our future in horoscopes.

Today be very careful because everything is set to work against you. Mistakes will turn into disasters and expect to have an argument with someone you really care about. Mars is ascending in your orbit and that means you are susceptible to losing it big time. Watch out! How will this change your behaviour?

Today you will have a great day and meet someone special. Everyone will want to help you out and finally appreciate your skills. The moon in Jupiter means your luck is endless today so expect to come into some money! How will this affect your behaviour?

Write a typical horoscope entry for this week to yourself.

....

....

....

....

....

....

....

....

PLTS objective: Develop a confident approach to challenges.

Draw a timeline for your life from birth until now with all the main events.

Now carry it on to 2050 and put in expected events. You have just predicted your future!

The Competency Curriculum Toolkit © Jackie Beere, Helen Boyle and Crown House Publishing Ltd

EMOTIONAL INTELLIGENCE (2) - SELF-BELIEF AND SOWING SEEDS OF OPTIMISM - CONTINUED

PLTS objective: Develop a confident approach to challenges.

SEEING IS BELIEVING ...

Create a visual picture in your mind of yourself at your most brilliant. Describe it to your group. Think of a saying that will remind you of it any time you need it. For example, 'Strong and indestructible' or 'Brilliant and beautiful'. Keep saying it over and over to yourself when you think of this picture.

Now create a superhero figure that can represent you when you are feeling that good. Draw it as a cartoon figure and draw a speech bubble with the saying in it too. Stick all of your group's characters onto a piece of large card and present your Power Team to the class.

HOW DID I DO?

What do we mean by self-belief?

....

....

....

Teacher's notes: What sort of thinker are you?

Resources: Lined/plain paper.

ACTIVITY
10
PROJECT 1 1 HOUR

PLTS objective

By the end of this lesson students will extend their thinking and develop metacognition.

Get excited!

Are you a more creative or logical thinker? The teacher poses questions about how we might approach different tasks and initiates discussion about how we think when we are learning.

Main learning activities

Students will complete a worksheet to review the two halves of their own brains.

The teacher needs to reinforce that students should be aiming to grow their whole brains. We all have preferences but our brain can be more powerful if we use both the logical and creative halves.

How did I do?

Some jobs lean towards having a logical or creative type brain—which careers use a blend of both? Students should set themselves one challenge to help them grow their whole brain and record it in their Tracker Pack.

Examples to grow your whole brain and be a golden thinker …

Try writing your name with the hand you don't normally write with.

Make a list of the jobs you have to do today and tick them off as you complete them.

Sit quietly on your own for fifteen minutes and listen to your own body and breathing.

Listen to a piece of music you have not heard before.

Learn to count to ten in a new language.

Bake a cake following the recipe and timings carefully.

Subject links

Learning to Learn
Study Skills

WHAT SORT OF THINKER ARE YOU?

ACTIVITY
10
PROJECT 1 1 HOUR

PLTS objective: To extend your thinking and develop metacognition.

GET EXCITED!

What sort of thinker are you? Are you more of a creative or logical thinker? We know that we can be clever in many ways, but what about the way we think when we are learning. If you had a jigsaw puzzle to do what would you do first? What do you do when you have a new computer or mobile phone—read the instructions or try it out until you get it right?

MAIN ACTIVITY

If you can make the logical and creative parts of your brain work well together when they need to then that makes your brain very powerful.

Tick some of these that you like:

Logical	Creative
Writing	Ideas
Logic	Intuition
Numbers	Daydreams
Analysing	Sport
Reading	Playing music
Sequencing	The big picture
Language	Rhythm
Detail	Colour
Spelling	Imagination

These two halves need to work together to make our brains work really well. For example, when we are doing a jigsaw puzzle we sort out the pieces using colour and shape but we have to think about the 'big picture' and imagine how it all fits together to get it right.

PLTS objective: To extend your thinking and develop metacognition.

To help understand the way your brain works answer these questions 'yes' or 'no':

1. I organise facts and material well.
2. I work step by step.
3. I can be impatient.
4. I read instructions before starting.
5. I like to work things out on paper.
6. I like working on my own.
7. I like to make lists.
8. I can concentrate well.
9. I like reading.
10. I enjoy working with numbers.

> More 'yes' than 'no'? You may be more of a logical thinker.

Now answer these questions 'yes' or 'no':

11. I prefer variety and excitement.
12. I like to doodle a lot.
13. I love trying out new ideas.
14. I think of creative solutions.
15. I like new experiences.
16. I just try out ideas as I go along.
17. I prefer to flick through a magazine starting at the back.
18. I make decisions based on gut feelings.
19. I find it hard to concentrate quite often.
20. I prefer art to reading and Maths.

> More 'yes' than 'no'? You may be more of a creative thinker.
>
> If you have a fairly equal number of yes/no answers you are in the middle, which is an excellent place to be because you are using all of your brain for learning!

PLTS objective: To extend your thinking and develop metacognition.

LEARNING HEALTH CHECK

Using *all* of your brain can make you more clever, so once you know which way you tend to think watch out for these health warnings.

Top tips for whole brain learning:

- Be open to trying new approaches.
- Don't get bogged down in detail.
- Practice working well with others.
- Vary your learning styles and habits to keep your creative brain working.
- Don't forget details—one step at a time.
- Make yourself do some planning and prioritising in advance.
- Avoid procrastination (putting things off until the last minute!).
- Avoid distraction and distracting others.
- Don't rush in without thinking.
- Read instructions and check work when finished.
- Plan deadlines and check them out.

TASK

Think of a job or career you would like. How would you use your logical and creative thinking in this role?

Now decide which is the most useful.

What sort of careers do creative thinkers have?

What sort of careers do logical thinkers have?

What sort of career could you have if you were good at both?

HOW DID I DO?

Write a statement to describe yourself as a thinker. Think of one challenge to set yourself to grow your brain and record it in your Tracker Pack.

....

....

Teacher's notes: Putting your PLTS into practice

Resources: Lined/plain paper, access to ICT, coloured pens, coloured paper.

PLTS objective

By the end of these lessons students will identify questions about learning, carry out research and communicate their PLTS learning.

Get excited!

The teacher should make clear that trying new things can help grow the whole brain.

Main learning activities

Students will plan and carry out their own research into preferred styles of learning and will present their findings to the rest of the class.

Students will use their teamwork skills to approach this task and the teacher should encourage students before they begin to establish what the success criteria should be for the presentations and agree on what each presentation should include—the worksheet aids this process.

Students will offer each others' presentations praise and advice to help develop their peer-assessment skills and provide effective feedback.

Optional learning tree display work

Students can create 'leaves' for their class learning tree by drawing around their hands and writing on them what they have learnt from project Brain Breakthrough—looking through their Tracker Packs should jog their memories! The hands can then be stuck onto the learning tree on the wall as a way of reviewing and recording their progress.

How did I do?

Students should review their Tracker Pack ratings of themselves.

Subject links

Learning to Learn
Study Skills
English/literacy
ICT

PUTTING YOUR PLTS INTO PRACTICE

PLTS objective: Identify questions about learning, carry out research and communicate your learning.

ACTIVITY
11
PROJECT 1   5 HOURS

GET EXCITED!

Fold your arms. Now fold them the other way. How does that feel?

Your brain enjoys doing things in certain comfortable ways. It also likes learning in its own way.

Each brain is very individual, like your thumbprint. However, if you understand and practice lots of ways to learn you will expand your brain power.

MAIN ACTIVITY

GROUP RESEARCH PROJECT

Find out more about learning styles so that you can grow your brain power. Get into groups and allocate roles and tasks, negotiate with your teacher a timeframe and deadline for this research task. Your task is to create a presentation about a chosen learning style or one of the Smarts to deliver to the group. You must also choose a piece of music to go with your presentation that inspires you to learn. Your presentation must include:

- Methods of learning.
- Activities that will help learning.
- Examples of famous people that demonstrate this learning style.
- Your chosen inspirational song.

PLTS objective: Identify questions about learning, carry out research and communicate your learning.

As you listen to the presentations fill in a box like this for each group:

> What was good about it?
>
> What constructive advice can you give to make it even better?
>
> How well did *you* contribute to your group's effort?

How has your brain become smarter? Create a learning map that shows everything you now know about your brain. Then answer this quiz:

- What is your learning style?

  ....

- How can you become a better learner?

  ....

- Why do you need to be emotionally intelligent?

  ....

- How can you control your moods?

  ....

- Why does it help to think positively?

  ....

Write three targets to make your brain smarter.

1. ....

2. ....

3. ....

CREATE A LEARNING TREE

Trace around your hand onto coloured paper, cut it out and write down what you have learnt from project Brain Breakthrough on the hand. Stick your hand on the learning tree on the wall in the classroom.

Project 2: Fair Trade

Activity No.	Activity Overview	PLTS Competence Objectives	Outcomes	Further Subject Opportunities	
1 **Estimated time** **2 hours**	**What is fair?** Students will explore the term *fair* and progress to explore the term *fair trade* and investigate the work of the Fairtrade Foundation. Students will research the impacts of fair and unfair trade. A useful website to support this work is www.fairtrade.org.uk. PLTS focus: T and P	■ To increase your understanding. ■ To cooperate with others to agree ways of achieving a definition of the terms *fair trade* and *unfair trade*. ■ To develop empathy with other people's situations from countries around the world. ■ To work to and meet deadlines.	■ Students will take part in a discussion about what is meant by the term *fair*. ■ Students will take part in a discussion about fair trade and the impacts of the Fairtrade Foundation. ■ Students will carry out their own research into unfair and fair trade and present their findings to the rest of the class. ■ Students will create their own definition for the terms *fair trade* and *unfair trade*.	Citizenship Geography English/Literacy Maths/ Numeracy ICT	
2 **Estimated time** **2–3 hours**	**Market research** Students will work in a team to create a questionnaire to gather consumer opinions and knowledge about fair trade products. PLTS focus: T, L and P	■ To cooperate with others as a team leader or a team member to investigate fair trade. ■ To develop your teamwork skills. ■ To develop your creative thinking skills.	■ Students will work as part of a team to carry out their research into consumer opinions about fair trade. ■ Students will create a questionnaire to gather consumer opinions about fair trade. ■ Students will feedback their teamwork efforts.	Citizenship English/Literacy MFL Geography History RE Maths/ Numeracy ICT	

Activity No.	Activity Overview	PLTS Competence Objectives	Outcomes	Further Subject Opportunities
3 **Estimated time** **3–4 hours**	**Product research** Students will undertake a research assignment to investigate the farming, refinement, production and distribution of a fair trade product. They will compare this against the unfair trade of the same product. Students will also investigate the social and economic impacts of fair trade pricing on the countries and the standards of living of people in those countries. Students will explore the environmental impacts of importing such products to the UK. Students will present their findings back to the class. Teachers should consider the grouping of students for this activity, e.g. higher ability students may be grouped together and focus on more difficult products like cotton. Lower ability students may be grouped together and focus on easier products like bananas. PLTS focus: T, L and P	■ To develop empathy with other people's situations from countries around the world. ■ To cooperate with others as a team leader or a team member to investigate a fair trade product. ■ To develop your creative talents and utilise your preferred learning styles. ■ To present your findings in an imaginative and informative way. ■ To develop your communication skills. ■ To manage information to research, evaluate and increase your own understanding. ■ To work to and meet deadlines.	■ Students will work as part of a team to carry out their own research into the farming, refinement, production and distribution of a fair trade product. ■ Students will research into the social and economic impacts of fair trade pricing on the countries and the standard of living of people in those countries. ■ Students will research into the impacts of unfair trade and include this in their final class presentation. ■ Students will work together to create a presentation aimed at a young teen audience to present findings of key facts, figures and information learned.	Citizenship Geography English/Literacy ICT Maths/ Numeracy

4 Estimated time 2 hours	Spend, spend, spend (1)		Citizenship Business Studies Maths/ Numeracy Literacy ICT
	Students will consider how the country is governed financially. They will explore the work of the Treasury and the Chancellor of the Exchequer. They will look at how revenue is created by taxation and how the budget is used to raise the rate of sustainable growth. Students will explore how they would prioritise sector spending of public money to run the country. PLTS focus: P, L and T	To manage information to research, evaluate and increase your own understanding about how the country is run. ■ To work to and meet deadlines. ■ To cooperate with others either one-to-one or in a team. ■ To develop awareness of how being an active citizen contributes to the working of our community.	■ Students discuss the terms *debt* and *interest*. ■ Students to discuss in their teams the impact on government spending (and the budget/sector spending) for countries paying interest from debt. ■ Students will take part in a class discussion to increase their knowledge of the work of the Treasury, the Chancellor of the Exchequer, taxation as revenue and the annual budget. ■ Students will identify sectors of public spending and use a spreadsheet to handle data-performing equations and to produce a graph or chart. ■ Students will create a report aimed at a professional audience to justify the reasons for their spending allocation. ■ Students will compare their ideas to actual spending by the current government.

Activity No.	Activity Overview	PLTS Competence Objectives	Outcomes	Further Subject Opportunities
5 **Estimated time 2 hours**	**Spend, spend, spend (2)** Students will work independently using information gathered and discussed in the last activity to create a report on how they would prioritise spending in the UK and give consideration to emergency funding. Students should be provided with the opportunity to present their work using ICT and spreadsheets. Students will be given opportunities to use self- and peer-assessment skills. PLTS focus: T, L and P	■ To increase your creative thinking skills. ■ To work more independently and organise your own work. ■ To cooperate with others as a team leader or a team member. ■ To work to and meet deadlines. ■ To reflect on the progress you have made and review how you can develop effective data-handling skills.	■ Students will identify sectors of public spending and use a spreadsheet to handle data performing equations and to produce a graph or chart. ■ Students will create a report aimed at a professional audience to justify the reasons for their spending allocation. ■ Students will compare their ideas to actual spending by the current government. ■ Students will offer praise and advice to each other.	Citizenship Maths/ Numeracy Literacy ICT
6 **Estimated time 4 hours**	**Import and export** Students will work in small teams to investigate which countries import and export goods and products. Students will be encouraged by their teacher to review and reflect on their team-working practices and how they are developing as team leaders and team players. Consideration should be given on how they might still improve teamwork activities. PLTS focus: T, L and P	■ To manage information to research, evaluate and increase others' understanding about import and export. ■ To work more independently and organise your own work. ■ To cooperate with others as a team leader or a team member. ■ To reflect on your teamwork and the part you have played in your team.	■ Students will identify where in the world products are grown and exported. ■ Students will work in teams to conduct research into countries which import and export different products. ■ Students will review their work as a team. ■ Students will offer each other praise and advice.	Literacy ICT Maths/ Numeracy Citizenship Geography

7 **Estimated time** **2 hours**	**Create your own product** Working in small groups students will undertake an enterprise activity where they will design, source and promote a fair trade product. They will work out profit/loss and determine a price for the product. They will vote as a class to pick one product from each class to sell on a fair trade market stall. Any money made will be donated to the Fairtrade Foundation or a world charity of the students' choice. PLTS focus: T, P and L	■ To cooperate with others as a team leader or a team member. ■ To work to and meet deadlines. ■ To develop effective data-handling skills. ■ To develop original ideas to completion, considering elements of risk or uncertainty. ■ To increase your independent learning skills. ■ To develop your creative thinking skills. ■ To develop your ability to reflect on success and manage disappointment.	■ Students will create a prototype/design for a product using fair trade ingredients or produce. ■ Students will produce a profit/loss spreadsheet model to show costs and anticipated revenue. ■ Students will produce advertising for their product, e.g. posters, radio jingles, TV adverts. ■ Students will produce an information leaflet or three-fold brochure about their product. ■ Students will present their product concept with promotional materials to the class. ■ Students will participate in a class vote for the best product and make the product to sell on a fair trade market stall.	Citizenship Enterprise Technology Maths/Numeracy Art ICT Music English/Literacy Geography
8 **Estimated time** **5 hours**	**Take your product to market** Using the product the class voted for students will work in small groups and undertake an enterprise activity where they will design, source and promote a fair trade product. They will organise themselves to make sure the whole class covers the advertising, sales, production and marketing of the product.	■ To work to and meet deadlines. ■ To develop original ideas to completion, considering elements of risk or uncertainty. ■ To cooperate with others as a team leader or a team member. ■ To increase your independent learning skills. ■ To develop your creative thinking skills.	■ Students will create a fair trade product to sell at a fair trade market stall. ■ Students will produce advertising for their product, e.g. posters, radio jingles, TV adverts. ■ Students will produce an information leaflet or three-fold brochure about their product.	ICT Maths/Numeracy Citizenship Enterprise Technology Art Music English/Literacy Geography

Activity No.	Activity Overview	PLTS Competence Objectives	Outcomes	Further Subject Opportunities
	Students will sell their product at a fair trade market stall. Any money made will be donated to the Fairtrade Foundation or a world charity of the students' choice. PLTS focus: T, P and L		■ Students will sell their fair trade product.	
9 **Estimated time 1 hour**	**How did we all do?** Using the product the class voted for students will work in small groups and undertake an enterprise activity where they will design, source and promote a fair trade product. They will organise themselves to make sure the whole class covers the advertising, sales, production and marketing of the product. Students will sell their product at a fair trade market stall. Any money made will be donated to the Fairtrade Foundation or a world charity of the students' choice. PLTS focus: T, P and L	■ To develop your ability to reflect on success and manage disappointment. ■ To develop your ability to set yourself meaningful learning targets.	■ Students will complete a project evaluation to review progress against the PLTS competencies and set targets for themselves in their next project. ■ Students will practise giving praise and advice.	Literacy Citizenship

Curriculum links

These curriculum links are taken from the QCA programmes of study for English, Geography, Design and Technology, Citizenship and PSHEE. Further information and links can be found at http://curriculum.qca.org.uk/key-stages-3-and-4/index.aspx.

These have been chosen as the most relevant to the work described in the project and may help teachers who are planning the delivery of the whole KS3 curriculum.

English AT 1 (Speaking and Listening)

Level 4: Pupils talk and listen with confidence in an increasing range of contexts. Their talk is adapted to the purpose: developing ideas thoughtfully, describing events and conveying their opinions clearly. They listen carefully in discussions, making contributions and asking questions that are responsive to others' ideas and views. They adapt their spoken language appropriately and use some of the features of standard English vocabulary and grammar.

Level 6: Pupils adapt their talk to the demands of different contexts, purposes and audiences with increasing confidence. Their talk engages the interest of the listener through the variety and liveliness of both vocabulary and expression. Pupils take an active part in discussions, taking different roles and showing understanding of ideas and sensitivity to others. They demonstrate their knowledge of language variety and usage effectively and use standard English fluently in formal situations.

Level 8: Pupils maintain and develop their talk purposefully in a range of contexts. They structure what they say clearly, using apt vocabulary and appropriate intonation and emphasis. They make a range of contributions that show they have listened perceptively and are sensitive to the development of discussions. They use standard English confidently in a range of situations, adapting as necessary.

Exceptional Performance: Pupils select and use structures, styles and registers appropriately, adapting flexibly to a range of contexts and varying their vocabulary and expression confidently for a range of purposes and audiences. They initiate and sustain discussion through the sensitive use of a variety of contributions. They take a leading role in discussion and listen with concentration and understanding to varied and complex speech. They show assured and fluent use of standard English in a range of situations and for a variety of purposes.

There are also links to English AT 2 (Reading) and AT 3 (Writing).

Geography

The key concepts include interdependence (exploring the social, economic, environmental and political connections between places and understanding the significance of interdependence in change); physical and human processes (understanding how sequences of events and activities in the physical and human worlds lead to change in places, landscapes and societies); environmental interaction and sustainable development (understanding that the physical and human dimensions of the environment are interrelated and together influence environmental change, and exploring sustainable development and its impact on environmental interaction and climate change); and cultural understanding and diversity (appreciating the differences/similarities between people, places, environments and cultures to inform their understanding of societies and economies, and appreciating how people's values and attitudes differ and may influence social, environmental, economic and political issues, and developing their own values and attitudes about such issues).

Design and Technology

The key concepts underpinning the study of design and technology include designing and making (the aesthetic, environmental, technical, economic, ethical and social dimensions and impacts on the world, exploring how products have been designed and made in the past, how they are currently designed and made, and how they may develop in the future) and cultural understanding (understanding how products evolve according to users' and designers' needs, beliefs, ethics and values and how they are influenced by local customs, traditions and available materials, and exploring how products contribute to lifestyle and consumer choices). In addition, the key processes offer the essential skills and processes that pupils need to learn to make progress. Pupils should be able to generate, develop, model and communicate ideas in a range of ways, using appropriate strategies; respond creatively to briefs, developing their own proposals and producing specifications for products; apply their knowledge and understanding of a range of materials, ingredients and technologies to design and make their products; and use their understanding of others' designing to inform their own.

Citizenship

Level 2: Pupils describe how things might be improved through the actions that they or others might take. They begin to recognise that all people have needs and wants and can identify the difference between the two. They begin to explore what is fair and unfair in different situations.

Level 3: Pupils recognise that issues affect people in their neighbourhood and wider communities in different ways. They investigate issues and find answers to questions using different sources of information provided for them. They present their ideas to others and begin to acknowledge different responses to their ideas. They discuss and describe some features of the different groups and communities they belong to. They identify different kinds of rights and understand that rights can conflict. They begin to recognise some features of democracy and know that people have a say in what happens locally and nationally. They identify what could be done to change things in communities and plan some action. They take part in decision-making activities with others on citizenship issues, in contexts that are familiar to them.

Level 4: Pupils explore a range of sources of information to engage with topical and controversial issues, including where rights compete and conflict. They identify different and opposing views and can explain their own opinion about what is fair and unfair in different situations. They develop research questions to explore issues and problems and begin to assess the impact of these for individuals and communities. They use what they find out to make informed contributions in debates. They begin to explain different ways in which people can participate in democracy through individual and collective actions and how they can change things in communities and wider society. They show an understanding of democracy by making connections with their knowledge and experience of representation and taking action in the local community.

Level 6: Pupils are aware of the diversity of opinions on topical and controversial issues and describe some of the influences that shape those opinions. They decide on appropriate research strategies and develop questions to investigate issues. They explore and interpret different sources of information and begin to assess these for validity and bias. They develop informed arguments, taking account of diverse viewpoints, and challenge assumptions or ideas as they explore them. They use their findings to present a persuasive case for a particular course of action, giving reasons for their view. They negotiate their role, and plan and undertake courses of action with others. They consider a range of scenarios (from local to global) where there are inequalities and explain how different kinds of rights need to be protected, supported and balanced. They show understanding of interdependence, describing interconnections between people and their actions in the UK, Europe and the wider world.

PSHE Economic Wellbeing and Financial Capability

The range and content of economic wellbeing and financial capability studies should cover the various opportunities in learning and work and changing patterns of employment (both local and global), introduce a range of economic and business terms, and consider social and moral dilemmas about the use of money. The key concepts covered include capability (becoming critical consumers of goods and services) and economic understanding (understanding the economic and business environment as well as the functions and uses of money). Key processes for students include enterprise (different approaches to working with others, problem solving and action planning and demonstrating and applying an understanding of economic ideas). The curriculum should provide opportunities for pupils to use case studies, simulations, scenarios, role play and drama to explore work and enterprise issues; engage with ideas, challenges and applications from the business world; explore sources of information and ideas about work and enterprise; and make links between economic wellbeing and financial capability and other subjects and areas of the curriculum

PSHE Personal Wellbeing

Pupils should understand the concept of risk (developing the confidence to try new ideas and face challenges safely, individually and in groups) and explore ideas about relationships (understanding that relationships affect everything we do in our lives and that relationship skills have to be learnt and practised; understanding that people have multiple roles and responsibilities in society and that making positive relationships and contributing to groups, teams and communities is important; and understanding that relationships can cause strong feelings and emotions). The essential skills and processes that pupils need to make progress with include critical reflection (to reflect critically on their own and others' values and on personal strengths, achievements and areas for development; to recognise how others see them and give and receive feedback; to identify and use strategies for setting and meeting personal targets in order to increase motivation; to reflect on feelings and identify positive ways of understanding, managing and expressing strong emotions and challenging behaviour; to develop self-awareness by reflecting critically on their behaviour and its impact on others). In developing relationships and working with others pupils should be able to use social skills to build and maintain a range of positive relationships; use the social skill of negotiation within relationships, recognising their rights and responsibilities and that their actions have consequences; use the social skills of communication, negotiation, assertiveness and collaboration; value differences between people and demonstrate empathy and a willingness to learn about people different from themselves; and challenge prejudice and discrimination assertively.

Enterprise

In order to help learners understand enterprise and develop entrepreneurial characteristics, they should have opportunities across the curriculum to take personal responsibility for their own actions through an enterprise process that involves four stages: (1) tackling a problem or need—students generate ideas through discussion to reach a common understanding of what is required to resolve the problem or meet the need; (2) planning the project or activity—breaking down tasks, organising resources, deploying team members and allocating responsibilities; (3) implementing the plan—solving problems, monitoring progress; and (4) evaluating the processes—reviewing activities and final outcomes, reflecting on lessons learned and assessing the skills, attitudes, qualities and understanding acquired.

Global Dimension and Sustainable Development

This extract from QCA Citizenship materials shows how the Fair Trade project can cover this element:

A curriculum for the 21st century should encourage learners to be aware of global issues. Learners should evaluate information and events from a global perspective. By exploring the connections between the local and the global, they can also realise that it is possible to play a part in working towards solutions to challenges, such as climate change and global poverty. The global dimension incorporates global citizenship, conflict resolution, diversity, human rights, interdependence, social justice, sustainable development and values and perceptions.

Teacher's notes: What is fair?

Resources: Lined paper, optional access to ICT/internet.

PLTS objective

By the end of this lesson students will increase their understanding of how to reflect, question and evaluate information.

Knowledge objective

By the end of this lesson students will be able to define *fair trade*.

Get excited!

The starter is a quotation taken from *Macbeth* that can be used with students to engage them in an open questioned debate about fairness. Prompt students to consider that what appears good could also be evil—things are not always what they seem.

Main learning activity

Students work in pairs to respond to statements about what is fair. This paired work will involve discussion and promote thinking skills. Students will be developing their competencies for teamwork and effective participation by discussing with others the questions about fairness. They will have to justify their ideas through discussion with a partner and evaluate their own ideas. This leads students to create a definition of fair trade and what it means. The research activity part of this lesson could be done by using the internet or books. Websites such as http://www.fairtrade.org.uk provide a good starting point.

Teachers can challenge and extend all students, especially Gifted and Talented students, by announcing during the course of this activity that budget cuts have to be made and now there is less money to spend — students would then need to employ other PLTS like self-management and creative thinking in revising their initial spending decisions.

How did I do?

The plenary provides teachers with the opportunity to check students' understanding of fair trade and the definitions that they have created.

Importantly, in a competency-based curriculum, assessment is focused on the process of learning, i.e. not simply what the students have learnt but *how* they have learnt.

Students should be able to describe how competent they have been in this lesson at questioning, reflecting and evaluating information.

How well have they worked with others?

Subject links

Geography
English/Literacy
Citizenship
ICT
Maths/Numeracy

WHAT IS FAIR?

PLTS objective: Generating ideas, evaluating actions, research and questioning.

GET EXCITED!

What do we mean by *fair trade*? 'Fair is foul and foul is fair' was chanted by the witches in *Macbeth*. What do you think it means? What do we mean by *fair*? Fair play … Fair dos … Fair enough … Can you think of any other expressions that include *fair*?

MAIN ACTIVITY

1. Working in pairs, use a tick or cross to respond to these statements:

- It's not fair to steal. ☐

- If I hit you, it's fair for you to hit me. ☐

- I forgot my homework so it was fair that I had to stand in the corner for the rest of the lesson. ☐

- It was fair that the whole class got a detention because we were noisy. ☐

- If people bomb us, so it's only fair that we bomb them. ☐

- I helped at home with the washing up so it's only fair that I get some new trainers. ☐

- If I lived in a country where I was poor because I couldn't get a job, it would be fair for me to be able to come to a country where I could earn some money. ☐

- These statements are very fair. ☐

WHAT iS FAIR? – CONTiNUED

PLTS objective: Generating ideas, evaluating actions, research and questioning.

2. Now write lots of definitions of *fair*.

....

....

....

....

....

....

....

Finish these sentences:

i. It's rained all summer so it's fair that

....

ii. I eat healthy food so it is not fair that

....

iii. I try to be kind to my sister but it's so unfair that she

....

Make up three more.

....

....

....

WHAT IS FAIR? – CONTINUED

PLTS objective: Generating ideas, evaluating actions, research and questioning.

3. Write three definitions of what *fair trade* might be.

   ....

   ....

   ....

4. Write three definitions of what *unfair trade* might be.

   ....

   ....

   ....

5. Now research on the internet or using books to check out your answers.

HOW DID I DO?

Define *fair trade* and *unfair trade*.

How did you think, evaluate and question in this lesson?

....

....

....

....

How well have you worked with others?

....

....

....

....

....

	Rate your skills 1–5
Thinking	
Questioning and researching	
Evaluating	

Teacher's notes: Market research

Resources: Lined paper, optional use of ICT/internet.

ACTIVITY **2** *PROJECT 2 2-3 HOURS*

PLTS objective

By the end of this lesson you will have participated effectively as a team.

Knowledge objective

To develop your knowledge about fair trade products and how to design questionnaires.

Get excited!

The starter is a word association game that will involve all students participating at the start of the lesson and reviewing their ideas of the word *fair*. Students take it in turns to say out loud a word they associate with the word *fair*.

Main learning activity

Students will establish good questioning techniques and spend time assigning team roles so that everyone participates.

Students will learn about fair trade through investigative research either using books, the internet or handouts provided by the teacher.

Try websites like http://www.fairtrade.org.uk. This will assist students in developing a questionnaire to help them develop their independent learning competency.

Students will organise themselves so each team member has a specifically assigned role and use this strategy to help them develop their teamwork competency.

Each team must present their team's work and take this opportunity to develop their communication and presentation techniques.

How did I do?

Students reflect on how well they worked in a team and how well their team performed.

The teacher should encourage them to state what worked well and analyse why things went well and look at how any mistakes can be learnt from in the future.

Subject links

Geography
History
Religious Studies
Citizenship
English
ICT
MFL
Maths/Numeracy

MARKET RESEARCH

PLTS objective: Work effectively in a team, empathise with other cultures.

GET EXCITED!

Find out what other people know about fair trade. Do a word association game with the whole class that starts off with the word *fair*.

MAIN ACTIVITY

If the answer is, 'Yes, we have no bananas', what is the question? Discuss the difference between open and closed questions and their usefulness for surveys: How old are you? How are you old? Do you like bananas? What do you like about bananas? What makes a good question when you are a researcher?

Form a team to achieve the next task—appoint a team leader, timekeeper, notetaker, includer and listener. In your teams create ten questions for a questionnaire about fair trade. Conduct the survey on fair trade and gather your results. Analyse them. Present your findings to the class.

HOW DID I DO?

Did you find out what people think about fair trade and why?

How well did you perform in your team?

....

How well did your team perform and why?

....

How could your team improve?

....

Teacher's notes: Product research

Resources: Lined/plain paper, sugar paper and coloured pens. ICT and internet access is recommended for this lesson. Alternatively print out information sheets using websites like: http://www.fairtrade.org.uk, http://www.fairtrade.net, http://www.traidcraft.co.uk or http://www.maketraidfair.com and/or put together a book box from your school library containing relevant reading materials.

Time: 3–4 hours. This suggested timeframe will allow students time to fully investigate their fair trade product, prepare and deliver their presentation.

PLTS objective

By the end of this lesson you will have worked successfully as part of a team. You will have used a variety of methods for finding out information about fair trade. You will develop your communication skills.

Knowledge objective

By the end of this lesson you will have developed your knowledge about a fair trade product.

Get excited!

Students create newspaper headlines illustrating the power of successful teamwork—encourage the imaginative use of alliteration.

At the start of this lesson students should review what their role is in their team:

'My role is … and it will make the team work brilliantly if I…'

Main learning activities

The teacher should allocate each team a fair trade product to investigate such as chocolate, bananas, flowers, coffee, tea, clothes or wine.

The students need to plan how to carry out their work and make sure that when they present their findings to the rest of the class they have found out how their product is farmed, refined, produced and distributed.

Students should choose how to present their findings and be ready to explain what and how they have learnt about their product, and how they have worked together.

How did I do?

Students should offer each other praise and advice on their final presentations and reflect on how well they have each worked as part of a team to complete the task.

Subject links

Geography
English/Literacy
ICT
Citizenship
Maths/Numeracy

PROJECT 2 - FAIR TRADE
PART 1 - PRODUCT RESEARCH

ACTIVITY
3
PROJECT 2 3-4 HOURS

PLTS objective: To work successfully as part of a team, to manage information effectively, to demonstrate excellent communication skills.

GET EXCITED!

Create two or three newspaper headlines that show the power of successful teamwork, e.g. 'Gold medal for British rowing team' or 'Local village wins first prize in Britain in Bloom competition'.

....

....

....

What is your role in the team?

My role is ....

and it will make the team work brilliantly if I ....

MAIN ACTIVITY

The objective of this exercise is to increase your knowledge about a fair trade product and meet your competency objectives. Get into the same teams formed for Activity 2. Choose a product to focus on (e.g. chocolate, bananas, flowers, coffee, tea, clothes, wine). Investigate your product. How it is farmed? How it is refined? How it is produced? How it is distributed?

Present your findings aimed at a young teen audience as either a leaflet, PowerPoint presentation, newspaper article, poster or mind-map. Your team will need to explain what you have done and what you have learnt throughout this process.

HOW DID I DO?

What did I do well in my team? ....

Even better if ....

The Competency Curriculum Toolkit © Jackie Beere, Helen Boyle and Crown House Publishing Ltd

PART 2 -
ASSESSMENT OF OUTCOME

ACTIVITY 3
PROJECT 2 1 HOUR

PLTS objective: To work successfully as part of a team, to manage information effectively, to demonstrate excellent communication skills.

GET EXCITED!

Make three positive comments from listening to other groups' presentations relating to the competency objective, reflecting on what excellent teamwork is and how to become a better team player.

MAIN ACTIVITY

Praise and advice. As a group, write down *three good things* about each group presentation based on these headings:

Communication
Teamwork
Learning

Now write down *three pieces of advice* about each group presentation based on these headings:

Communication
Teamwork
Learning

PART 2 -
ASSESSMENT OF OUTCOME

PLTS objective: To work successfully as part of a team, to manage information effectively, to demonstrate excellent communication skills.

Now do the same for your own group:

Communication
Teamwork
Learning

Now do the same for yourself about your own performance and then discuss with the group:

Communication
Teamwork
Learning

HOW DID I DO?

What have you learnt from this lesson?

....

....

What makes groups work well?

....

....

How could your role have been better?

....

....

Teacher's notes: Spend, Spend, Spend (1) – How the government spends your money

ACTIVITY
4
PROJECT 2 · 2 HOURS

Resources: Lined paper, calculators. Access to ICT and the internet is recommended for these lessons.

PLTS objective

By the end of this lesson you will have worked successfully as part of team and developed your ability to reflect and question information.

Knowledge objective

By the end of this lesson you will have increased your knowledge about government spending.

Get excited!

Give students the two-minute task of using their imagination to consider how they would spend a million pounds if they ran the country and what would they spend it on. Encourage every student in the room to contribute one thing to this discussion.

Main learning activities

Teacher-led questions and information about who runs the country, what is taxation and how revenue is spent.

Who runs the finances for the country? (Chancellor of the Exchequer)

What different taxes are there? (income tax, road tax, VAT, council tax, corporation tax, inheritance tax, etc.)

Write a list of the things our taxes are spent on. (Education, health, defence, public services, transport, industry, agriculture, public order, housing and environment, etc.)

Students need to assign themselves roles in their teams (see Activity 3) and then complete the group task of how they would spend the country's budget.

How did I do?

Students should write a short speech to help them analyse their group's spending and how government groups should decide what to spend money on.

Students feedback their team's decisions including their reasoning and share how well they worked as a team.

Subject links

ICT
Maths/Numeracy
Business Studies
English/Liteacy
Citizenship

SPEND, SPEND, SPEND (1) - HOW THE GOVERNMENT SPENDS YOUR MONEY

PLTS objective: Researching and communicating information using ICT as a team.

GET EXCITED!

In pairs, imagine you are the Prime Minister and you had a million pounds to spend on this country. How would you spend it?

MAIN ACTIVITY

Who runs the finances for the country? What types of different taxes are there? Write a list of the things our taxes are spent on and put the list in order of priority.

Form your teams and decide on the roles for the next activity. You will need a team leader, timekeeper, notetaker, includer and listener.

As a group, decide how much you would spend on each of the sectors below. Divide the £557 billion pounds that the UK government spends based on your priorities.

	Sector	£billion
1		
2		
3		
4		
5		
6		
7		
8		
9		
10		
Total		557

SPEND, SPEND, SPEND (1) - HOW THE GOVERNMENT SPENDS YOUR MONEY - CONTINUED

PLTS objective: Researching and communicating information using ICT as a team.

There are ten sectors to choose from:

1. Social protection (unemployment benefit, pensions, child support, etc.)

2. Public services (recreation and leisure)

3. Housing and environment

4. Public order and safety

5. Industry, agriculture, employment and training

6. Defence

7. Education

8. Transport

9. Health (NHS)

10. Personal social services (social services, care of children, elderly, etc.)

ACTIVITY 4
PROJECT 2 PAGE 3

PLTS objective: Researching and communicating information using ICT as a team.

HOW DID I DO?

How should government groups decide what to spend money on?

....

....

....

....

....

....

How well did you work in a team?

....

....

....

....

....

....

Better if

....

....

....

....

....

Teacher's notes: Spend, Spend, Spend (2) – Making decisions about money

Resources: Lined paper, calculators. Access to ICT is recommended for this lesson.

PLTS objective

By the end of this lesson you will have developed your competency for independent learning and creative thinking.

Knowledge objective

By the end of this lesson you will be able to use a spreadsheet to handle data-performing equations and be able to produce a graph or chart.

Get excited!

Using the flood scenario students are to imagine what they would spend when 100,000 people are affected by flooding. Set a strict time limit for this starter and feedback. The teacher should link this activity to the spending plans the students made in the previous lesson and explain how emergencies like floods can change everything.

Main learning activities

Using previous lesson material students should use their team's data to create a report that they must deliver to the class.

This can be an optional teamwork or individual work task.

Teachers will need to familiarise themselves with basic addition, subtraction and multiplication spreadsheet formulas to guide students through this activity.

Teachers will need to familiarise themselves with using a spreadsheet to create a chart or graph.

Students will learn about how formulas can be used within spreadsheets to handle information more effectively.

How did I do?

Students must be encouraged to evaluate how well they have managed and handled data. What have they done well and what tips should they remember for future data-handling activities?

Evaluate with praise and advice their role in teams, if applicable.

Subject links

ICT
Maths/Numeracy
Citizenship
Literacy

SPEND, SPEND, SPEND (2) - MAKING DECISIONS ABOUT MONEY

PLTS objective: To reflect on how spending decisions are made and how this data can be communicated.

GET EXCITED!

Floods devastate the country and 100,000 people are affected. How much money will you give to help them?

MAIN ACTIVITY

1. In your groups review your spending decisions and create a report to deliver to a professional audience about the decisions you have made. Use a spreadsheet to handle data-performing equations and produce a graph or chart. Deliver your report to the class.

2. Compare your report with the way the money was spent by the government over the period of one year (see table below).

Sector	£billion
Social protection	161
Public services	59
Housing and environment	22
Public order and safety	33
Industry, etc.	21
Defence	32
Education	77
Transport	20
Health	104
Personal social services	28
Total	**557**

HOW DID I DO?

On a separate sheet write a short budget speech to justify your sector spending.

How well did I manage information using ICT?

How well did my group work?

Teacher's notes: Import and export

Resources: Card, scissors, coloured pens, lined/plain paper. Access to ICT is recommended for these lessons.

PLTS objective

By the end of this lesson you will successfully relate to others in a team. You will also be able to use a variety of methods for finding out and presenting your ideas.

Knowledge objective

By the end of this lesson you will be have developed your knowledge about imported and exported products.

Get excited!

Set a strict one-minute time limit for students to complete the starter activity. Students may only have a few answers to these questions at the start of this lesson but they can be encouraged to reflect again later in the lesson.

Main learning activities

Students will discuss named products and determine if they think they are imported or home-grown. Fair trade products will assist in this discussion work.

Websites like http://www.fairtrade.org.uk may be helpful to support this task.

Students should make sure that when they work in teams they assign team roles to everyone and select an appropriate method to present their research on debt in developing countries.

Teachers should encourage team leaders to feedback to the class how they are working, how they can improve their team effort, and discuss any problems they are facing as a team and how they might be best resolved.

How did I do?

Teachers should question students – How well have you worked in a team? How do you know?

Use praise and advice feedback to review PLTS competence learning.

Subject links

Maths/Numeracy
Citizenship
Geography
Literacy
ICT

iMPORT AND EXPORT

PLTS objective: To communicate well as a team, to manage and present information about importing and exporting products.

GET EXCiTED!

Think of three reasons why some countries are rich and some countries are poor.

1. ....

....

....

2. ....

....

....

3. ....

....

....

IMPORT AND EXPORT - CONTINUED

PLTS objective: To communicate well as a team, to manage and present information about importing and exporting products.

MAIN ACTIVITY

Which products do we import? Tick the correct box (some may be both!).

Produced	Home-produced	Imported
Bananas		
Pineapples		
Tea		
Coffee		
Chocolate		
Oil		
Rice		
Potatoes		
Apples		
Computers		

1. Look at your list of imported products. Which countries do they come from?

....

....

....

....

....

....

....

....

....

The Competency Curriculum Toolkit © Jackie Beere, Helen Boyle and Crown House Publishing Ltd

IMPORT AND EXPORT
- CONTINUED

PLTS objective: To communicate well as a team, to manage and present information about importing and exporting products.

2. What makes a country rich?

....

....

....

3. What makes a country poor?

....

....

....

4. If we couldn't import *any* products from other countries because of climate change, how would it affect you?

....

....

....

Now think about countries which are not as rich as the UK and consider why. Assign group members their roles again (see Activity 2). Your group task is to:

• research/discuss why some countries have a debt

• research what we mean by third world debt

• find out about how countries pay interest on that debt

• present a campaign using leaflets, posters or PowerPoint presentations arguing for and against the campaign to drop third world debt.

Teacher's notes: Create your own product

Resources: Lined/plain paper, coloured pens, fair trade ingredients. Access to ICT is recommended for this lesson.

Time: 2 hours. Note: this activity can be as big as you want it to be. This is the pinnacle of the project and if time permits students could hold a fair trade market at their school. The only limit to this task is your and your students' imaginations!

PLTS objective

By the end of this lesson you will work effectively as part of a team and manage information.

Knowledge objective

You will increase your understanding of how to create and market a fair trade product.

Get excited!

Allow students one minute to reflect on what fair trade products they themselves use and consider where they are from in the world.

Main learning activities

Encourage students to take on different roles in their teams for this activity so they can develop their competence for different ways of relating to others.

Students will design, create, produce and market a fair trade product (e.g. cookies, smoothies, sweets, t-shirts).

How did I do?

Students feedback their ideas and outline how their product is fair trade.

Students describe how well they have worked as a team so far to complete this task.

Subject links

Technology
Art
Citizenship
Maths/Numeracy
ICT
Geography
English/Literacy
Enterprise
Music

PROJECT 2 - FAIR TRADE
CREATE YOUR OWN PRODUCT

PLTS objective: Take part in a team and contribute to the development of a product, generate ideas, plan time and resources effectively.

GET EXCITED!

What fair trade products do you use/eat? Where do they come from?

MAIN ACTIVITY

Assign the team roles (see Activity 2) and complete the following tasks: create a fair trade product using fair trade ingredients or produce (e.g. cookies, jewellery, clothes, smoothies, sweets) then create a marketing campaign.

HOW DID I DO?

How is our product fair trade?

....

....

How did we work together as a team?

....

....

Teacher's notes: Take your product to market

Resources: Access to ICT, lined/plain paper, coloured pens.

PLTS objective

By the end of these lessons you will work as part of a team effectively. You will manage your own time and work independently.

Knowledge objective

By the end of this lesson students will create one of the following: a letter to the Prime Minister, a product information leaflet, a PowerPoint presentation about fair trade, a newsletter aimed at primary school children or a letter to a local supermarket.

Get excited!

Encourage all students to participate in the review of how their team worked well in the last lesson. Consider the top tips for excellent teamwork and display these to help students through the next activity.

Main learning activities

Students should divide up their team's workload and carry out their team roles to create marketing and publicity material for their fair trade market stall.

If time allows students could produce their fair trade products to sell to fellow class members.

How did I do?

Students should offer praise and advice to each other about their fair trade products, marketing campaign and teamwork.

Subject links

Music
Art
ICT
English/Literacy
Geography
Technology
Maths/Numeracy
Citizenship
Enterprise

TAKE YOUR PRODUCT TO MARKET

PLTS objective: Evaluate your own and others' work, communicate and collaborate effectively with others.

GET EXCITED!

Think of a single sentence to say why your team worked the best in the previous lesson.

MAIN ACTIVITY

Create a fair trade stall for your team to sell your products. Visit other stalls and see which products you would like to buy.

As a follow up to the fair, the team should choose from the following activities:

1. Write a letter to the Prime Minister telling him about fair trade.

2. Produce an information leaflet for your product.

3. Create a PowerPoint presentation about fair trade.

4. Produce a newspaper article or newsletter reporting on the outcomes of the fair trade project for primary school children.

5. Write to a local supermarket giving reasons why they should stock fair trade produce.

HOW DID I DO?

Evaluate one team's product at the fair.

....

....

State what they did well and why it was effective.

....

....

State what they could have improved and how.

....

....

Teacher's notes: How did we all do?

Resources: Lined paper.

PLTS objective

By the end of this lesson you will develop your understanding of how there are several ways you can make changes and you are able to celebrate success and manage disappointment.

Knowledge objective

By the end of this lesson you will have developed your ability to self-assess and peer-assess others.

Get excited!

Give students one minute to think over the qualities that make up an excellent product.

Main learning activities

Students rate each other and their own performance in relation to the fair trade product task.

How did I do?

All students should be able to say one thing they have learnt about themselves and share tips for successful teamwork.

As a result of this project students should be able to suggest how their learning will affect their future choices and behaviour.

Students should record outcomes from this project in their Tracker Pack.

Subject links

English/Literacy
Citizenship

HOW DID WE ALL DO?

ACTIVITY 9
PROJECT 2 1 HOUR

PLTS objective: Self- and peer-assessment.

GET EXCITED!

What qualities would make the best fair trade product out of all those you have seen?

....

....

....

....

....

MAIN ACTIVITY

Each group reminds the class of the name and slogan of their product.

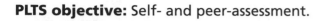

PRAISE AND ADVICE

Write a praise comment on each of the following headings for each group.

	Insert a grade from 1–5 and add a comment
Learning about fair trade	
Communicating ideas	
Teamwork	

Write an advice comment on each of these headings for each group:

	Insert a grade from 1–5 and add a comment
Learning about fair trade	
Communicating ideas	
Teamwork	

ACTIVITY
9
PROJECT 2 PAGE 2

PLTS objective: Self- and peer-assessment.

Write a praise comment on each of these for your own group:

	Insert a grade from 1–5 and add a comment
Learning about fair trade	
Communicating ideas	
Teamwork	

Write an advice comment on each of these for your own group:

	Insert a grade from 1–5 and add a comment
Learning about fair trade	
Communicating ideas	
Teamwork	

HOW DID WE ALL DO?
– CONTINUED

PLTS objective: Self- and peer-assessment.

Now fill in the boxes for your own performance.

Praise:

	Insert a grade from 1–5 and add a comment
Learning about fair trade	
Communicating ideas	
Teamwork	

Advice:

	Insert a grade from 1–5 and add a comment
Learning about fair trade	
Communicating ideas	
Teamwork	

HOW DID I DO?

Say one thing you have learnt about yourself as a member of the team.

....

....

Say one thing you are going to do differently as a result of the fair trade project.

....

....

Project 3: Money, Money, Money

Activity No.	Activity Overview	PLTS Competence Objectives	Outcomes	Further Subject Opportunities
1 **Estimated time** **1 hour**	**The cost of living** The students will explore financial terminology and create a wall display to embed learning. They will investigate their knowledge of simple everyday costs. For fun, students will think of music that relates to money such as songs by ABBA or Pink Floyd.	■ To discover how much you know about money already. ■ To consider how much simple everyday things cost. ■ To make a connection between money and the real world.	■ Students will take part in a discussion about money and increase their vocabulary about financial terminology. ■ Students will create a piece of display work for the wall using these terms.	Maths Music Literacy Citizenship PSHEE
2 **Estimated time** **3 hours**	**Planning budgets** Students create a hypothesis then plan a budget for a variety of activities, such as feeding a family of four, by finding out what the costs are and compiling a budget.	■ To improve your knowledge of how to manage your own money. ■ To undertake independent research about what items cost. ■ To cooperate with others as a team member or a team leader.	■ Students will develop an awareness of the costs of modern living, such as buying a house and how to plan a budget. ■ Students will present their budgets to spread the learning about different areas across the class.	Maths Citizenship English (Speaking and Listening) PSHEE D and T
3 **Estimated time** **1–2 hours**	**Is money good or evil?** This activity is a Community of Enquiry for students to consider the philosophical aspects of money. This includes reading from the Bible and reflecting on abstract aspects of how we view money. This activity will focus on listening, questioning and speaking skills.	■ To reflect on why we consider being rich is important. ■ To listen to each other and respond with empathy. ■ To ask appropriate questions at a higher level	■ Students will hold a controlled discussion that gives the whole class a chance to talk about issues around money and wealth. ■ This Community of Enquiry will be based around the principles of Philosophy for Children. ■ Students will develop their questioning and listening skills.	English RS Citizenship

Activity No.	Activity Overview	PLTS Competence Objectives	Outcomes	Further Subject Opportunities
4 **Estimated time** **3 hours**	**Create a currency** Students will create their own currency notes after researching the history of money. They will then create prototype designs for their currency. The class should vote on the best design. The class can then use the favoured currency to promote citizenship activities in the class, e.g. 50 notes could be printed and students would earn this class money by completing tasks such as picking up litter or refreshing displays. This can be cashed in with vouchers or linked to the school reward system.	■ To research from a range of sources about currencies. ■ To participate in a scheme of rewards using your chosen class currency. ■ To work as a team to create your design.	■ Students will design their own currency having investigated other examples and discovered the codes and conventions. ■ Students will give feedback about each others' designs. ■ Students will take part in a vote to judge the best design in the class and use the currency to promote citizenship activity in the class.	D and T Citizenship Maths History PSHEE
5 **Estimated time** **1–2 hours**	**Manage your money** Students will complete a questionnaire to assess their 'money profile' to help them develop good habits with their future finances. Students will then analyse the pros and cons of terms they first discussed in Activity 1.	■ To understand your attitude to money. ■ To reflect on how you can make money work well for you. ■ To review the financial vocabulary with reference to your own money profile. ■ To set yourself targets for developing your skills.	■ Students will develop their self-awareness about their spending profile so that they can manage their finances well. ■ They will produce a list of the pros and cons of important aspects of money management following on from reviewing their own profile.	Maths Citizenship PSHEE

6	Advertising		English
Estimated time 3 hours			Citizenship
			ICT
			D and T
	Students will look at advertising and how it targets audiences to create a need. The context is the 2008/9 'credit crunch' and why people may have developed debts.	■ To understand the codes and conventions of advertising and how it impacts on the target audience.	■ Students will take part in a discussion about the media messages they receive every day and how they relate to spending habits. Students will analyse various advertisements that will demonstrate how audiences are targeted to create need.
	Students will consider how much is spent on advertising compared to manufacturing.	■ To develop creative ideas that will help people manage money effectively.	■ Students will examine media codes and conventions that they can then apply to creating a leaflet or website using what they have learnt about financial management to teach younger students useful lessons.
	This activity will complete the project by students creating a piece of communication, such as a website, leaflet or lesson for younger students, that summarises their learning.	■ To review your learning and progress in this project.	

Curriculum links

This project has obvious links with the PSHE Economic Wellbeing and Financial Capability programme of study. A selection of the most relevant statements is given below from http://curriculum.qca.org.uk/key-stages-3-and-4/index.aspx. In addition, some links to the Maths programme of study are included with relevant levels expected. More links can be found at the above website.

PSHE Economic Wellbeing and Financial Capability

The Money, Money, Money project has obvious links with this programme of study. Key concepts covered include capability (exploring what it means to be enterprising, learning how to manage money and personal finances, becoming critical consumers of goods and services) and an economic understanding of the functions and uses of money. Key processes include financial capability (pupils should be able to manage their money, understand financial risk and reward, explain financial terms and products, and identify how finance will play an important part in their lives and in achieving their aspirations).

The range of subjects covered should include the personal review and planning process; personal budgeting, money management and a range of financial products and services; risk and reward, and how money can make money through savings, investment and trade; how businesses use finance; and social and moral dilemmas about the use of money. The curriculum should provide opportunities for pupils to use case studies, simulations, scenarios, role play and drama to explore work and enterprise issues and make links between economic wellbeing and financial capability and other subjects and areas of the curriculum.

Mathematics

Activity 2 (Planning budgets) can help to cover various areas from the mathematics programme of study. These include the key concepts of competence (applying suitable mathematics accurately within the classroom and beyond—which requires fluency and confidence in a range of mathematical techniques and processes that can be applied in a widening range of familiar and unfamiliar contexts, including managing money, assessing risk, problem solving and decision making—and communicating mathematics effectively); the applications and implications of mathematics (understanding that mathematics is used as a tool in a wide range of contexts, which includes using mathematics as a tool for making financial decisions in personal life and for solving problems in fields such as building, plumbing, engineering and geography, internet security, weather forecasting, modelling changes in society and the environment, and managing risk, e.g. insurance, investments and pensions, and engaging in mathematics as an interesting and worthwhile activity); and critical understanding (knowing that mathematics is essentially abstract and can be used to model, interpret or represent situations but recognising its limitations and scope, e.g. mathematical skills are needed to compare different methods of borrowing and paying back money, but the final decision may include other dimensions, such as comparing the merits of using a credit card that promotes a particular charity with one offering the lowest overall cost). The curriculum should provide opportunities for pupils to develop confidence in an increasing range of methods and techniques; work on sequences of tasks that involve using the same mathematics in increasingly difficult or unfamiliar contexts; work on open and closed tasks in a variety of real and abstract contexts that allow them to select the mathematics to use; work on problems that arise in other subjects and in contexts beyond the school (e.g. representing and analysing data in Geography, using formulas and relationships in Science, understanding number structure and currency exchange in Modern Foreign Languages, measuring and making accurate constructions in Design and Technology, and managing money in economic wellbeing and financial capability, or conducting a survey into consumer habits,

planning a holiday budget, designing a product, and measuring for home improvements); work on tasks that bring together different aspects of concepts, processes and mathematical content; work collaboratively as well as independently in a range of contexts (this includes talking about mathematics, evaluating their own and others' work and responding constructively, problem solving in pairs or small groups and presenting ideas to a wider group); and become familiar with a range of resources, including ICT, so that they can select appropriately.

There may also be opportunities to assess pupils at Level 4 and Level 5.

King of Learning OBE

Teacher's notes: The cost of living

PLTS objective

By the end of this lesson students will have discovered how much they know about money already and how much simple everyday things cost.

Knowledge objective

By the end of the lesson students will know financial terms and what they mean.

Get excited!

Students will work with others to discover how much they know about money already and how much simple everyday things cost. If they don't have regular money they can consider what money they get and how they spend it through drawing the mind-map of what they spend from day to day.

Main learning activity

1. Money word wall display. Students can use dictionaries or computers to find out what the words mean then produce large displays of individual words to place around the classroom to create a word wall. Students can take it in turns to explain what each term means.

2. Money quiz. The quiz is intended to make students consider approximate costs for everyday items that may relate to them now or in the future. This activity could be done in pairs. The list of amounts can be adjusted according to current values.

3. Name three songs that have lyrics related to money. This is a fun activity where students can think of songs that mention money—and even sing them!

How did I do?

The plenary can check how many of the financial terms can be recalled by the students and what their relevance could be in their lives

Subject links

Maths
Music
Literacy
Citizenship
PSHE

THE COST OF LIVING

PLTS objective: To discover how much you know about money already, to consider how much simple everyday things cost and to make a connection between money and the real world.

GET EXCITED!

How much income do you have each week? Create a learning map of what you spend it on.

MAIN ACTIVITY

1. Money word wall display. See which of these terms you understand. Write associated words and images around each word for the wall display: credit, tax, wages, insurance, mortgage, currency, pension, loan, store card, interest, savings.

2. Money quiz. Estimate to the nearest amount—choosing from the box below.

    1. What is the minimum wage per hour?
    2. What is the single person's old age state pension per week?
    3. How much is family allowance for the first child per week?
    4. How much is the Education Maintenance Allowance that students get post-16 worth per week?
    5. How much does a passport cost?
    6. How much does the cheapest mobile phone cost?
    7. How much is a first class stamp?

Choose answers from this list:
£5
£60
£25
£28
£30
£80
50p

3. Name three songs that have lyrics related to money.

1. ....

2. ....

3. ....

Teacher's Notes: Planning budgets

Resources: Catalogues/internet, ICT access.

ACTIVITY 2 — PROJECT 3 · 3 HOURS

PLTS objective

To improve students' knowledge of how to manage their own money. Students will undertake independent research about what items cost and cooperate with others acting as a team member or team leader.

Knowledge objective

By the end of the lesson students will know costs for various objects and services.

Get excited!

The aim of the starter is to give students a warm-up of mental arithmetic that relates to saving. Thinking of creative ways to spend £50 will enable the teacher to compare the values and interests of students. Will any decide to donate to charity?

Main learning activity

The students work in teams to plan a budget for a holiday, house or other activities. The task begins with student teams guessing how much each task will cost and the teacher recording these estimates to compare at the end. The teacher could put these in rank order of most and least expensive and then return to this list at the end.

It is recommended that teams create their budgets in a spreadsheet using simple addition tools to do running totals. The budget will be presented as a list of items and a total amount to be spent.

Presentations of the budgets to the class could be followed by questions and suggestions about how each budget could be made more economical or generous.

Students will need two hours to research and write up then an hour for the class to present their budgets.

The activity can finish with reflection on the original estimates and seeing who got the closest to the final budgets.

How did I do?

Students state how they could make each of the purchases a bit cheaper or more expensive.

Subject links

Maths
Citizenship
English (Speaking and Listening)
PSHEE
D and T

PROJECT 3 - MONEY, MONEY, MONEY
PLANNING BUDGETS

PLTS objective: To improve your knowledge of how to manage your own money, to undertake independent research about what items cost and to cooperate with others acting as a team member or team leader.

GET EXCITED!

You save £5 a week for ten weeks. In one minute plan what you will spend it on.

MAIN ACTIVITY

In groups of four or five carry out the tasks below. Create a hypothesis … guess which will cost the most! Rank order them in terms of the most and least expensive.

Plan a budget for the following by finding out what the costs are and writing a list of what you will spend in your teams. You will need to research from catalogues and the internet to find out the prices for things. Make a list of everything you think you will need and price them up. Add up your total for the challenge and then present your budgets to the class.

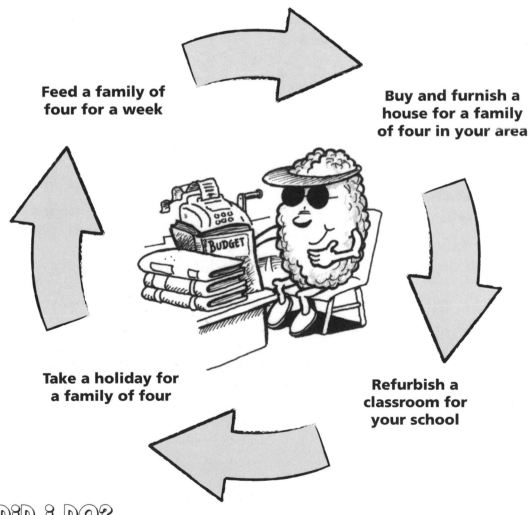

Feed a family of four for a week

Buy and furnish a house for a family of four in your area

Take a holiday for a family of four

Refurbish a classroom for your school

HOW DID I DO?

How you could make each of these a bit cheaper or more expensive?

Teacher's notes: Is money good or evil?

PLTS objective

Students will reflect on why we consider being rich important. They will listen to each other and learn to respond with empathy and to ask appropriate questions at a higher level. Students will develop their higher order and abstract thinking skills.

Get excited!

For the starter the students can consider what it means to be on the Rich List and whether money is always a good thing. They could guess who is the richest out of a number of celebrities or how much footballers earn each week.

This lesson is based on Philosophy for Children democratic Community of Enquiry conventions. These include:

1. The purpose is to discuss a concept or philosophy using open and curious questioning and supportive, focused listening.

2. Students sit in a circle to enhance concentration.

3. Students accept certain codes of conduct, which include listening to each other and participating.

4. Everyone is encouraged to contribute or ask questions.

5. Questions are encouraged to be controversial, contestable, open and philosophical.

6. Students take turns talking and are all responsible for mutual contributions.

7. There are no right and wrong answers.

8. Everyone respects the opinion of others and their right to express it.

However, the teacher can construct this according to their own context.

Main learning activity

The reading from the Bible that relates to the morality of making money is the parable of the talents (Matthew 25: 14–30). This reading provides the stimulus for a Community of Enquiry that follows the following plan.

In pairs students think of an open, controversial, philosophical question related to the parable (these questioning levels may need some preparation with students).

After two to three minutes one of the pairs writes their question on the board.

When all the questions are written on the board the class votes on which question they like best. Each student should have three votes so that they can vote for their own and other questions.

If there are two questions with an equal score then the students get another vote.

When the question has been chosen the Community of Enquiry can begin.

The winning question is read out by the pair that devised it and then expanded on. From then on anyone can take part in the discussion. Following on from the debate the further questions (see above) can become part of the enquiry.

Finally, the review question encourages students to make a list of what else matters in their lives.

How did I do?

Students make a list of what would become important if money became worthless.

Students should be encouraged to analyse how well they contributed to the debate by speaking and/or listening. The English Speaking and Listening APP (Assessment of Pupil Progress) model can be used to help teachers assess students and students assess their own performance in the discussion.

Subject links

English
RS/Citizenship

PROJECT 3 – MONEY, MONEY, MONEY
iS MONEY GOOD OR EViL?

PLTS objective: To reflect on why we consider being rich important, to listen to each other and respond with empathy and to ask appropriate questions at a higher level.

GET EXCiTED!

What is the Rich List? Name some very rich people that you know and write what they do on a Post-it note.

MAiN ACTiViTY

Read the parable of the talents from the Bible (Matthew 25: 14–30). Discuss in pairs a question that results from your discussion of that story. Each pair should write their question on the board. The class then chooses the question they wish to investigate in a Community of Enquiry. In a circle all students must discuss the chosen question and give their opinion or ask further questions.

COMMUNiTY OF ENQUiRY

Further questions for discussion in the enquiry:

- Does being rich make you happy?
- How does being rich make you happy?
- What else do you need to make you happy?
- How can being rich make you unhappy?
- If you won a million pounds how could it make you unhappy?
- Why don't animals need money?

HOW DiD i DO?

On a separate sheet make a list of what would become important if money became worthless.

Teacher's notes: Create a currency

Resources: Card, paper, coloured pens.

ACTIVITY
4
PROJECT 3 · 3 HOURS

PLTS objective

Students will research from a range of sources about currencies. Students will participate in a scheme of rewards using their chosen class currency and work as a team to create their own currency design.

Knowledge objective

By the end of the lesson students will know the history of currency and the features of notes and coins.

Get excited!

The starter aims to get the students thinking about what we mean by currency and the practical aspects of money.

Main learning activity

Students get into teams and research the history of currency and money using books or the internet. Following on from this the teams design and create their own currency notes and coins. When these are complete the class can examine each others' designs and choose one to use as a class currency through a class vote. This is an optional activity but could be fun to help students earn some of the class currency for community activities such as litter picking and display maintenance. The notes that are earned over a term could be cashed in for vouchers or linked to the school reward system.

How did I do?

Peer-assessment across the group can be used to assess the currency and choose the favourite to be used for the class currency.

Subject links:

D and T
Citizenship
History
Maths
PSHEE

CREATE A CURRENCY

ACTIVITY
4
PROJECT 3 · 3 HOURS

PLTS objective: You will research from a range of sources about currencies and participate in a scheme of rewards using your chosen class currency. You will work as part of a team to create your own currency design.

GET EXCITED!

Name as many currencies as you can think of and find out their exchange rate against the British pound.

MAIN ACTIVITY

In teams research the history of money and various currencies. Design your own currency—create a name for it, design a note and coins and create prototypes. Find some products and price them up in your currency.

Each group then chooses their favourite currency which then becomes the class currency. Fifty notes are produced and given out for jobs around the group (e.g. litter collection, display checking, giving out books, helping each other). The notes can be cashed in at the end of term for prizes or real money.

Teacher's notes: Manage your money

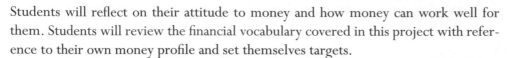

PLTS objective

Students will reflect on their attitude to money and how money can work well for them. Students will review the financial vocabulary covered in this project with reference to their own money profile and set themselves targets.

Main learning activity

This lesson is aimed at making students reflect on their own attitude to money and helping them manage money effectively. Teachers may need to adjust amounts in the money quiz depending on the school context. When the quiz is completed students can work out what their targets may be in the future in terms of making money work well for them.

How did I do?

The follow-up activity considers the pros and cons about certain aspects of money for *them* with their own money profile. For example, credit cards are fine if you are a saver but dangerous if you are a spender. The wall display of financial terms and their meanings (from Activity 1) will provide useful reference points for some of these questions.

Subject links

Maths
Citizenship
PSHEE

MANAGE YOUR MONEY

ACTIVITY
5
PROJECT 3   1-2 HOURS

PLTS objective: To understand your attitude to money, to reflect on how you can make money work well for you, to review the financial vocabulary with reference to your own money profile and to set yourself targets for developing your skills.

GET EXCITED!

Write on a Post-it note the three things that you most like to spend money on.

 ## MAIN ACTIVITY

What is your money personality—spender, saver or 'spaver'? Answer the questions in the pound and penny profile as honestly as you can. Tick the boxes that most apply to you:

Do you work for any of your income?	No	Sometimes	Yes
What is your total weekly income?	£0–5	£6–20	£21+
How much do you spend each week?	£21+	£6–20	£0–5
How much have you got in savings?	£0–10	£11–100	£100+
How often do you go shopping for yourself?	Once or more per week	Two or three times per month	Once a month
If you want something can you save up for it?	Never	Sometimes	Always
How much do you spend on clothes each month?	£50+	£11–50	£0–5
How much do you spend on music/multimedia each month?	£11+	£6–10	£0–5

MANAGE YOUR MONEY - CONTINUED

ACTIVITY
5
PROJECT 3 PAGE 2

PLTS objective: To understand your attitude to money, to reflect on how you can make money work well for you, to review the financial vocabulary with reference to your own money profile and to set yourself targets for developing your skills.

How much do you spend going out each week?	£11+	£6–10	£0–5
How much do you spend on food and drink each week?	£11+	£6–10	£0–5
Have you ever borrowed any money?	Often	Sometimes	Rarely
Do you pay back your borrowings?	Sometimes	Yes—eventually	Yes
What would you do if you were given £100?	Spend it straight away on stuff I want	Spend some and save some	Put it in a savings account
What would you do if you won a million pounds?	Buy a house, a car and have an expensive holiday	Go on a shopping spree, give some to charity and put the rest in a bank	Get advice from a financial advisor
Add up the ticks in each column			
Do you think you are a spender, saver or spaver (a bit of each)?	Spender	Spaver	Saver

Is this what you thought you would be? Set some targets for the future so that you can manage your budget.

MANAGE YOUR MONEY – CONTINUED

ACTIVITY
5
PROJECT 3   PAGE 3

PLTS objective: To understand your attitude to money, to reflect on how you can make money work well for you, to review the financial vocabulary with reference to your own money profile and to set yourself targets for developing your skills.

REVIEW

Fill in the financial pros and cons table with everything you know or can find out about these topics and how they relate to *your* profile:

	PRO	CON
Credit card		
Debit card		
Pension		
Mortgage for a house		
Renting a house		
Store card		
eBay purchases		
Bank account		
Income tax		
Internet shopping		
Loans		
Pawn shop		
Insurance		
Catalogue shopping		

Discuss each of these as a class and then prioritise them.

Teacher's notes:
Advertising – Creating a need or feeding a greed?

PLTS objective

Students will understand the codes and conventions of advertising and how this impacts on the target audience. Students will develop creative ideas that will help people manage money effectively, and students will review their learning and progress in this project.

Knowledge objective

By the end of the lesson students will know the codes and conventions of advertising that are used to target audiences and a create a need.

Get excited!

The purpose of this lesson is to relate what students have been working on to the real world of material temptation.

Main learning activity

Students can find or bring in advertisements for luxury goods and notice the prices—or lack of them! They can consider how persuasive messages are used to help target audiences who may want the product. During this lesson students will be able to analyse the codes and conventions of advertising such as the use of logos, copy and pictures, as well as varied fonts and colours to create emotive responses. This activity can refer back to the Brain Breakthrough project where students learnt about how the emotional brain works.

How did I do?

The final activity uses some of the knowledge about how the media targets us to create an effective communication that summarises all the learning from this project. For example, the use of colour and rhyming slogans makes the information easily memorised in the emotional brain. The artefact they produce can be a website, advert or prepared/planned lesson for younger students to help them learn about money.

If the teacher can organise the best projects to be delivered to younger students, and assessed by them for feedback to the young teachers, this will be an excellent form of peer-assessment for this project.

Finally, students can complete their praise and advice and Tracker Packs, assessing their progress in the PLTS competences during this project.

Subject links

English
Citizenship
ICT
D and T

ADVERTISING - CREATING A NEED OR FEEDING A GREED?

ACTIVITY 6 PROJECT 3 3 HOURS

PLTS objective: You will understand the codes and conventions of advertising and how it impacts on the target audience. You will develop creative ideas that will help people manage money effectively. You will review your learning and progress in this project.

GET EXCITED!

Look at a magazine or recall TV adverts that feed on our emotions and create a need for expensive items.

MAIN ACTIVITY

Analyse one magazine and choose ten adverts. Look at the prices of the products and find out or estimate what they may cost to manufacture. Looking at your pound and penny profile (see Activity 5) which products tempt you? What techniques are used to make us want expensive items such as cars, make-up, clothes and so on?

HOW DID I DO

In your team create one of the following to demonstrate what you have learnt from this project: (1) an advice website about money, (2) a leaflet for primary school children helping them to learn the essentials about money or (3) prepare a one-hour lesson for Year 6 students about money.

Project 4: Saving Planet Earth

Activity No.	Activity Overview	PLTS Competence Objectives	Outcomes	Further Subject Opportunities
1 and 2 **Estimated time** **5 hours**	**A story for the future** Reading *A Sound of Thunder* and reflecting on the way we are impacting on the future of our planet. **What are the problems?** Using focus cards for each group students research topics using key words and quotations. Presentations to the class demonstrate and embed learning for each topic.	■ Effective participation in the group reading of a text. ■ Reflective learning about the messages in the text. ■ Working effectively in a team to research the problems. ■ Deciding what are the crucial problems we face on planet Earth.	■ The students have an opportunity to explore a text written 60 years ago which demonstrates that concern about the planet is not something new. ■ The presentations about the problems facing the planet should be an excellent way of learning from each other. Each student will take notes during the presentations for the next activity.	English Science Geography Citizenship ICT PSHEE
3 **Estimated time** **3–5 hours**	**What are the solutions?** The focus is on finding solutions and communicating them to the group. The work is in pairs and takes the issues to a new level by producing a piece of communication that has been researched, e.g. a website, drawing or advertising campaign.	■ Creative thinking about how we can address the concerns about our planet. ■ Effective participation in making a persuasive case for action after assessing all viewpoints. ■ Independent enquiry into effective communication techniques.	■ Each pair or individual student will produce a communication focused on one aspect of the problems facing the planet. The communication must address a realistic solution.	Art English Science Geography ICT PSHEE

Activity No.	Activity Overview	PLTS Competence Objectives	Outcomes	Further Subject Opportunities
4 Estimated time 5 hours	**Get practical to save the planet** Linking back to understanding the emotional brain, this takes the practical and creative work a step further by working in groups to dramatise or use artistic interpretation to create a powerful impact on an aspect of Saving Planet Earth, e.g. drama, rap or photography. These will be demonstrated to the class and peer-assessed for impact.	■ Reflective learning on what they have found out about eco-issues and how to use it to persuade others to care. ■ Effective participation in a creative project with a team. ■ Self-managing to self- and peer-assess performance.	■ The outcome of this activity is to use a creative, artistic approach to communicating some of the issues that they have learnt about in this project. ■ The artefacts produced will be peer-assessed for impact as part of the development of an awareness of formative assessment techniques.	Art and Design Drama and Expressive Arts ICT and Multimedia English Music Science Geography PSHEE

Curriculum links

The links between this project and the KS3 National Curriculum shown below are by no means exhaustive. Virtually all of the Citizenship Attainment Target could have been included in this summary. We would also recommend that you study the cross-curricular dimensions in the National Curriculum, in particular those for Global Dimension and Sustainable Development. See http://curriculum.qca.org.uk/key-stages-3-and-4/cross-curriculum-dimensions/globaldimension/index.aspx.

More links can be found at the 2007 National Curriculum programmes of study at http://curriculum.qca.org.uk/key-stages-3-and-4/index.aspx by clicking on the 'subjects' tab. Enjoy!

Citizenship

There are too many links to the Citizenship Attainment Target, ranging from Level 1 to Exceptional Performance (EP) to include here. Follow the link to http://curriculum.qca.org.uk/key-stages-3-and-4/cross-curriculum-dimensions/globaldimension/index.aspx.

Science

At AT1 Level 4 students begin to relate their conclusions to patterns in data, including graphs, and to scientific knowledge and understanding. At AT1 Level 6 they communicate their conclusions using appropriate scientific language and communicate qualitative and quantitative data effectively using scientific conventions and terminology. At AT1 EP they communicate findings and arguments, showing their awareness of the degree of uncertainty and a range of alternative views.

At AT3 Level 5 pupils describe applications and implications of science, such as the uses of metals based on their specific properties or the benefits and drawbacks of the use of fossil fuels. At AT4 Level 6 they use abstract ideas or models, for example, sustainable energy sources; apply and use knowledge and understanding in unfamiliar contexts; describe evidence for some accepted scientific ideas; and explain the importance of some applications and implications of science, such as the responsible use of unsustainable sources of energy.

Geography

Level 4 students understand that people can both improve and damage the environment. They offer reasons for their own views about environmental change and recognise that other people may hold different views. They use primary and secondary sources of evidence in their investigations and communicate their findings using appropriate vocabulary. At Level 5 they understand some ways that human activities cause environments to change and demonstrate an awareness of the idea of sustainable development, also recognising the range of views people hold about environmental interaction and change. At Level 6 pupils recognise how conflicting demands on the environment may arise and describe and compare sustainable and other approaches to managing environments. They appreciate that different values and attitudes, including their own, result in different approaches to environmental interaction and change, identify potential bias in sources, present their findings in a coherent way using appropriate methods and vocabulary and reach conclusions that are consistent with the evidence. At Level 7 students understand that many factors influence decisions made about sustainable and other approaches to developing places and environments, and use this understanding to explain the resulting changes. They appreciate that the environment in a place and the lives of the people who live there are affected by actions and events in other places. They recognise that human actions, including their own, may have unintended environmental consequences and that change sometimes leads to conflict. At Level 8 they analyse different approaches to developing places and environments and explain the causes and consequences of environmental change, understand how the interaction between people and environments can result in complex and unintended changes, and understand and describe a range of views about environmental interaction. At EP pupils understand alternative approaches to development and their implications for the quality of life in different places. They assess the relative merits of different ways of tackling environmental issues and justify their views about these different approaches. They understand how considerations of sustainable development can affect their own lives as well as the planning and management of environments and resources, and illustrate this with a full range of examples.

ICT

At Level 4 pupils combine and refine different forms of information from various sources. They understand the need for care in framing questions when collecting, finding and interrogating information; interpret their findings, question plausibility and recognise that poor-quality information leads to unreliable results; and use ICT to present information in different forms and show they are aware of the intended audience and the need for quality in their presentations. At Level 5 students select the information they need for different purposes, check its accuracy and organise it in a form suitable for processing. They use ICT to structure, refine and present information in different forms and styles for specific purposes and audiences. At Level 6 they present their ideas in a variety of ways and show a clear sense of audience.

Design and Technology

The programme of study states the following should be covered: understand that designing and making has aesthetic, environmental, technical, economic, ethical and social dimensions, and impacts on the world and the needs of users and the problems arising from them (e.g. benefits for a minority or the majority, for the present or the future); assess products in terms of sustainability, to include researching and thinking about the use of renewable sources or exploring alternatives to less sustainable materials. This includes recognising that new materials are being developed all the time and understanding the tension between cost, the demands of the product and sustainability issues, such as minimising waste and reusing materials.

Teacher's notes: A story for the future

PLTS objective

Students will learn to effectively participate in a group reading of a text and reflect on the messages contained in the text.

Knowledge objective

By the end of the lesson students will know some of the ways man is endangering the planet.

Main learning activity

Read *A Sound of Thunder* (1952) by Ray Bradbury together. This can be downloaded as text from the internet through Wikipedia. Following on from the story students should list all the things we are doing to our planet now that may make a difference for our great-great-grandchildren.

How did I do?

For the plenary students can recall the story and relate it to the actions they have identified in the activity. They should demonstrate they can see the connections.

Subject links

English
Science
Geography
Citizenship
ICT

A STORY FOR THE FUTURE

PLTS objective: By the end of this activity you will participate in a group
reading of a text and reflect on the messages the text contains.

MAIN ACTIVITY

As a group read *A Sound of Thunder* by Ray Bradbury. This is
a science fiction short story about people travelling backwards
in time and breaking the rules. This scary story shows us how
our unthinking actions can change the world. Following on
from this story:

What are we doing to our planet now that could impact on our great-great-grandchildren's
lives? Write a list of everything you can think of and what its impact may be in the future.

....

....

....

What actions are we taking that may damage the future?

....

....

....

What could happen in the future?

....

....

....

....

....

....

....

Teacher's notes: What are the problems?

Resources: Internet access and/or book box, Post-it notes.

PLTS objective

Students will combine teamworking and research skills with being able to prioritise problems for planet Earth.

Knowledge objective

Students will find out about various aspects of current dangers to the planet.

Get excited!

Students should reflect on what makes their planet special using the Post-it notes. These can stay on the wall for reflection at the end of the lesson. The guidance from the teacher should be that students aim for quantity of ideas rather than quality, to develop creative thinking and move away from believing there are 'right' answers.

Main learning activity

For the team presentation on the problems for planet Earth, the teacher should provide a brief introduction on each topic and then give every team a research card (which can be photocopied from the focus cards below). The cards provide key words for their research and controversial statements to explore on each topic. The biggest challenge will be to pick out the most important aspect of the research area to report on back to the class. Research should be on the internet or through a book box created by the school library—or both.

Teachers may need to add key advice on research skills such as:

- Using search engines and key words.

- Only printing off a limited number of pages.

- Using a highlighter pen to edit printed pages.

- Noting down important quotes and who said them.

- Organising the research findings into a structure for the presentation to other students (e.g. What is the problem? What is the evidence for the problem? What are the expected outcomes? What is the main question that arises from our research?).

The success criteria for each presentation could be determined with the students (e.g. five minutes long, clear explanation of the problem and evidence for it, some facts and opinions about the topic). Each group has to finish their presentation with a major question that has arisen from their research.

Praise and advice

Each student should take notes during the team presentations then reflect on their notes and write praise and advice for each group.

How did I do?

Look back at the Post-it notes and put the six topics in order of priority to save the planet.

Subject links

English
Science
Geography
Citizenship
PSHEE
ICT

WHAT ARE THE PROBLEMS?

ACTIVITY
2
PROJECT 4   3 HOURS

PLTS objective: You will practise working effectively in a team to carry out research into the various problems facing planet Earth.

GET EXCITED!

In pairs write on a Post-it note three things you love about living on this planet compared to what it might be like to live on the moon.

MAIN ACTIVITY

In your group use the six focus cards (below) to plan research on your topic and prepare a five-minute presentation for the class to inform them about the facts and debates on your particular focus.

---

1. The energy gap

'150 experts say more nuclear power needed'

'In 2015 energy demand will exceed supply by 23% in UK'

'WWF says UK does not need nuclear power as we can't get rid of the waste'

'Oil to run out by 2100'

Key words
Fossil fuels
Combustion
Carbon dioxide
Sustainable/unsustainable
Renewable/non-renewable energy
Solar energy
Biomass energy
Wind energy
Tidal energy
Nuclear energy
Gigawatt
Energy saving/conservation

2. Nature under threat

'Pandas or people?'

'25% of land animals and plants to be extinct by 2050'

'Fen orchid to disappear—who cares?'

'Humans are causing the greatest mass extinction since the death of the dinosaurs'

Key words
Extinction
Conservation
Species
Habitat loss
Food chains and webs
Endangered
Red List
Adapt
Biodiversity
Ecosystem
Deforestation
Desertification

WHAT ARE THE PROBLEMS?
- CONTINUED

PLTS objective: You will practise working effectively in a team to carry out research into the various problems facing planet Earth.

3. Extreme weather

'Southern Europe to become a desert'
'Gulf Stream may stop—Britain to freeze'
'By 2100 the Earth could be warmer than for the last 10 million years'
'London to flood'

Key words
Carbon dioxide
Methane
Global warming
Climate change
Gulf Stream
Polar ice
Floods
Storms
Hurricanes
Typhoons
Monsoons
Drought
Desertification
Sea level rise

4. Poisoning the Planet

'The average American makes 20.4 tonnes of carbon dioxide but China makes the most'
'In some cities breathing the air is like smoking 20 cigarettes a day'
'900,000 tonnes of oil/year spilled into the oceans'

Key words
Carbon dioxide
Methane
Landfill
Pollution
Non-biodegradable
Toxic waste
Heavy metals
Litter
Chlorofluorocarbons (CFCs)
Acid rain
Industrialisation
Sewage
Asbestos
Carbon footprint
Food miles

WHAT ARE THE PROBLEMS?
- CONTINUED

PLTS objective: You will practise working effectively in a team to carry out research into the various problems facing planet Earth.

---

5. Waste and recycling
'Think globally, act locally'
'We would need 3.5 Earths if we all lived like Americans'
'Consumer societies are happier'
'Reduce, reuse, recycle'

Key words
Landfill
Metals
Glass
Plastics
Paper
Water
Composting
Conservation
Reforestation
Energy conservation
Food waste
Carbon footprint
Consumer culture
Exporting waste
Packaging

6. Over-population of the planet
'World population to rise by 50% in 40 years'
'China limits number of children'
'Large families are happy families'
'Three billion people live on less than 50p per day'

Key words
Birth rate
Death rate
Billions
Developed/developing countries
Poverty
Demographic change
Birth laws
Growth of cities/urbanisation
Consumerism
Limited resources
Food
Water
Famine
Energy demand
Resource wars

Typing the key words above into an internet search engine should produce lots of useful hits but also try these websites:

http://www.recyclenow.org
http://www. recycling-guide.org.uk
http://www.stopglobalwarming.org
http://tiki.oneworld.net
http://www.bbc.co.uk/climate
http://www.bbc.co.uk/nature/animals/conservation
http://www.direct.gov.uk/environmentandgreenerliving

PRAISE AND ADVICE

On a separate sheet, write a positive statement about each of the presentations and some advice about how it could be even better. Write three good things about your own work or presentation and write one thing that could have been better and say how.

Teacher's notes: What are the solutions?

ACTIVITY 3 PROJECT 4 3-5 HOURS

Resources: Access to the internet. Sugar paper and cardboard waste for the eco-home. It is important for students to be resourceful and plan what resources they need and request them from the teacher for the next lesson.

PLTS objective

Students will use prior learning from Activity 2 to develop a solution idea independently and to demonstrate effective learning about the environment.

Knowledge objective

Students will know how some of the challenges to the planet can be resolved.

Get excited!

The starter should make students consider the impact of the environment on their own future and how they need to think of some solutions. For example, to tackle the waste mountain we need to recycle our rubbish at home and at school. If we don't, the number of landfill sites will increase.

Main learning activity

Each activity will follow on from the previous group work but this is to be produced in pairs, so may make use of other groups' research materials. Teachers can decide if they feel students would like to tackle different topics for this activity.

Several hours will be needed to produce the solutions and it is suggested that students create their own success criteria for their chosen activity, for example:

Activity	Success criteria
Create an eco-home	Should have at least five eco-features which can all be explained on the picture or model.
Scary weather survival pack	Should deal with three types of scary weather and include facts and pictures.
'Which animals shall we save?' website	A home page and three link pages, designed in colour with varied fonts, text boxes and pictures.

How did I do?

After several lesson hours the students will have completed their solution project and met their success criteria. They may wish to self-assess the outcomes and assess their PLTS progress. Each item will be presented/demonstrated to the group and explained. Peer-assessment can then take place and students can fill in their Tracker Pack for the work on this part of the project.

The completed materials could be used to create a display in the school foyer.

Subject links

Art
English
Science
Geography
ICT
PSHEE

PROJECT 4 - SAVING PLANET EARTH
WHAT ARE THE SOLUTIONS?

PLTS objective: You will use your creative thinking skills to consider how we can address the concerns about our planet and effectively participate in making a persuasive case for action after assessing all viewpoints.

ACTIVITY
3
PROJECT 4   3-5 HOURS

GET EXCITED!

Think of three reasons why *you* should find some solutions to these problems.

1. ....

2. ....

3. ....

MAIN ACTIVITY

Choose one of the following to complete in pairs:

Present a case for limiting the birth rate to one child per family

Create an advertising campaign called 'How can we stop the lights going out?'

Make a scary weather survival pack

PLANET EARTH SOLUTIONS

Produce a leaflet showing how you can reduce your carbon footprint

Produce a website called 'Which animals shall we save and how?'

Create an eco-home – a drawing or model

Teacher's notes: Get practical to save the planet

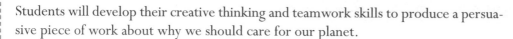

PLTS objective

Students will develop their creative thinking and teamwork skills to produce a persuasive piece of work about why we should care for our planet.

Get excited!

Connecting to Project 1 (Brain Breakthrough) this starter is a reminder about what turns on the emotional brain. In pairs students can take two minutes to think of novel ways to get their message across (e.g. telling jokes, creating cartoons, posters, air balloons with banners, rap/pop song, children's book, campaign with TV adverts).

Main learning activity

This is an opportunity to plan and create a piece of live communication that will make an impact. It links the subject to the creative arts such as drama, art and music. Each group must: (1) agree an activity, (2) make a list of resources needed and how to get them and (3) plan how to complete it in the timescale two hours.

What will we produce?	What is the wow factor that will make people think about the planet?	Who will do what?	Resources needed

How did I do?

Students should self-evaluate their production then peer-assess each group's presentation with a particular focus on the emotional impact of the message. A class discussion about what did and did not work well would be useful here. In addition the teacher can lead the class to reflect on how what they learnt in the different stages of this project (research, project and creative production), what the challenges were at each stage and how well they worked together.

At the end of this activity students should complete their Tracker Pack to self-assess how they have progressed through the Saving Planet Earth project in the PLTS.

Subject links

Art and Design
Drama
ICT
English
Music
Science
Geography
PSHEE

PROJECT 4 – SAVING PLANET EARTH
GET PRACTICAL TO SAVE THE PLANET

ACTIVITY
4
PROJECT 4   5 HOURS

PLTS objective: You will reflect on what you have researched about eco-issues. You will develop your teamworking skills in a creative project by putting together a case to persuade others to care for our planet.

GET EXCITED!

Our emotional brains love colour, rhythm, rhyme, humour, novelty, stories, challenge, love and relevance. How can we persuade people to save the planet using these techniques?

MAIN ACTIVITY

In groups choose to create one of the following that will have a powerful impact on others:

- Create a recycled sculpture.
- Write a rap to save the future.
- Perform a drama of life in 2070.
- Use a digital camera to create a PowerPoint presentation of the threat to our planet.
- Create masks and perform a mime.
- Write a poem or story called 'Save the planet'.

Before you start write down the success criteria for your chosen activity. How will you know it's good?

Chosen activity	Success criteria

GET PRACTICAL TO
SAVE THE PLANET – CONTINUED

PLTS objective: You will reflect on what you have researched about eco-issues. You will develop your teamworking skills in a creative project by putting together a case to persuade others to care for our planet.

Demonstrate what you create to other classes and ask them to evaluate its impact on their awareness of issues relating to Save Planet Earth.

Score each others' efforts according to how much creativity they have used and how much it makes you think about the problems.

Peer-assessment sheet (mark out of 5)

	It made me think about the planet	All team members took part	It was explained clearly	It demonstrated creative thinking	Total score
Team 1					
Team 2					
Team 3					

The Competency Curriculum Toolkit © Jackie Beere, Helen Boyle and Crown House Publishing Ltd

PROJECT 4 - SAVING PLANET EARTH
GET PRACTICAL TO
SAVE THE PLANET - CONTINUED

PLTS objective: You will reflect on what you have researched about eco-issues. You will develop your teamworking skills in a creative project by putting together a case to persuade others to care for our planet.

	It made me think about the planet	All team members took part	It was explained clearly	It demon-strated creative thinking	Total score
Team 4					
Team 5					

Now complete your Tracker Pack for your own PLTS progress.

Section 3

PLTS Breakthrough Projects

These projects are group activities that are more loosely structured so students can apply a collaborative learning model to other topics. Students can eventually plan their own learning projects culminating in an externally assessed accreditation. Some of these projects are also suitable as homework tasks and have proved highly engaging and motivational for students.

Teacher's notes

These lessons are intended to embed learning and thinking skills in a group project which focuses on students observing the personal, learning and thinking skills (PLTS) as they work on an engaging group task with a clear outcome. They are useful when the competency-based projects have been completed and students have taken more responsibility for developing their PLTS. There are several ideas in this book but students are encouraged to create their own tasks and by the end of Year 8 plan their own projects and measure their own PLTS progression. In order to ensure the standard of activities is high the task plan includes a section for students to decide their success criteria for each task chosen. Points scored for each task can also be recorded and the teacher can decide how to record and reward group points scores.

Progression

From the planned projects in Year 7 to student-led projects in this section, the PLTS progression is the main aim of the competency curriculum. In order for us to construct a course that has an accredited outcome and measures the overall impact of the development of independent learning skills by the age of 14 it is suggested that the course culminates in entry for the AQA or Edexcel project. This is worth 0.5 GCSE and is a course where learners choose their own project to study as an individual or group. Students have to identify the PLTS to be developed, share the project outcome and evaluate their progress—this is an independent, self-directed project which is the perfect test of the development of the PLTS. We suggest that this could be taken in Year 9 at the appropriate level for the ability of the student, as a measure of progress in the ability to plan, assess and develop their personal, learning and thinking skills.

The first project is 'Communication Olympics' which may be suitable for students in Year 7 who need to focus on literacy. Some activities have been included to demonstrate how the PLTS and core skills can be delivered. The other projects have been tried and tested and proved to be very popular with students.

Project plan

- Review the PLTS.

- Students: choose two or three PLTS objectives and note them in your Tracker Pack.

- PLTS objectives: team leadership, team membership, creating ideas, communicating ideas, researching information, sorting information, motivating yourself, motivating others, meeting deadlines, giving good feedback, taking criticism, making mistakes, being optimistic, managing emotions, using a variety of learning styles, etc.—or make up your own by looking at the descriptions and statements in the Tracker Pack.

■ Form your teams and ensure you are working with different students for each project so that you can develop your interpersonal skills with different team members.

■ Review all the tasks in the PLTS Breakthrough Projects and spend five minutes deciding which tasks you will do, who you will do them with and completing the task plan at the end of this section.

■ When the project tasks are complete, each group will present their project to the class and review their progress in the PLTS. The teacher and students will assess the outcome of the group project.

COMMUNICATION OLYMPICS

The Communication Olympics project is aimed at developing the habits of excellent communication.

Spell well

Creative a spelling quiz programme like *Countdown*

– 6 points

Write well

Make a poster with the top ten tips for beautiful handwriting

– 5 points

Write a lesson plan for students in Year 7 to help them improve their literacy and communication skills

– 10 points

COMMUNICATION OLYMPICS

Story glory

Write and illustrate a group ghost story. Check it through for spelling and punctuation

– 10 points

Speak up for success

Create a children's magazine TV programme where you take the role of presenters

– 10 points

Word power

Find ten really difficult but useful words and learn how to use them to expand your vocabulary

– 5 points

LITERACY ACTIVITIES

PLTS objective

Communicate language ideas effectively and creatively

Skills objective

Use words for speaking and writing accurately

WRITE WELL

PLTS objective: teamwork, persistence, goal setting.

Skills objective: to write legible and beautiful handwriting.

GET EXCITED!

Write your signature with your wrong hand. Write it again—more beautifully. Get some feedback from a friend. Write it a third and fourth time and show improvement.

MAIN ACTIVITY

Handwriting clearly is a crucial skill and I can get better at it by practising. Copy out this sentence clearly, evenly and neatly on lined paper. Take your time.

Discuss why so many adults find it hard to write clearly. Do we need to be able to handwrite if we always use computers? Think of examples of when we need to write by hand. Make a mind-map showing why you need good clear handwriting as an adult.

As a team look at all the handwriting completed above by placing all the papers into the centre of the table. Examine all the examples and make a list of ten top tips for beautiful handwriting (e.g. make sure capital letters are bigger than lowercase letters).

In pairs write out these top tips on a large piece of paper with a thick felt-tip pen.

Get into the habit of writing clearly. Close your eyes and imagine a beautiful golden pen with a lovely, free-flowing red ink. Your hand wraps around it snugly and feels comfortable. As you write it produces attractive, even writing that is like a work of art. The pen moves smoothly and softly over the paper and never makes any mistakes.

Do this every time you write for three weeks and it will transform your handwriting!

Now copy this saying into your book in your favourite colour ink:

> *People will forget what you say,*
> *People will forget what you do,*
> *But people will never forget the way you made them feel.*

Choose the best written piece in your team and place it on the front desk for the handwriting section of the Communication Olympics. The teacher will award bronze, silver and gold medals.

Fill in your Tracker Pack for the PLTS for this lesson.

COMMUNICATION OLYMPICS

SPELL WELL

PLTS objective: teamwork, leadership, creative learning.

Skills objective: spell more accurately.

GET EXCITED!

Why do you need to spell if you can use a spellcheck on the computer? What are the secrets of spelling well?

MAIN ACTIVITY

Create a crazy spelling quiz. As a team make up a list of the twenty spellings you find tricky and would like to spell accurately because they would be useful (e.g. *discipline*, *chaos*). Write them out neatly and accurately.

Swap your list with another team. Teach each other the spellings by testing and re-testing each other in pairs. After ten minutes your team is prepared.

Each group has to be tested by the teacher on the list they have learnt in the Spelling Olympics. The group with the most correct spellings wins gold, then silver and bronze medals.

HOW DID YOU LEARN?

What methods did you use to teach and learn the spellings? Were there any common rules that were helpful? Write a help sheet for 7-year-olds giving them top tips for developing good spelling habits.

Fill in your Tracker Pack with the PLTS progress for this lesson.

COMMUNICATION OLYMPICS
WORD POWER

PLTS objective: take responsibility, make mistakes, generate ideas.

Skills objective: learn new words that can be used in speech and writing.

GET EXCITED!

- What do these words have in common—*cyberbunny, facepinch, craxle, snoogle*?

- How do you rate your vocabulary—poor, good or brilliant?

MAIN ACTIVITY

- Write down your favourite words that you use a lot.

- Have some fun with words—make up some crazy words that mean the same as *beautiful.* Use these words to make up a nonsense rhyme as a pair.

- Expand your vocabulary. Pick up a book, newspaper article or dictionary and select your favourite words to write down. Make sure you know what they mean.

- Woooooooo! word game. In a group of four look at all the words you have found and make a wordlist. Pass this list around the group with each member of the group putting the word into a sentence. The whole group supports each member to use the word properly. Share your best sentences with the class.

- Play Scrabble in groups of four.

- Learn a new word every day and use it as often as possible. It doesn't matter if it's not quite right straight away. Here some good ones to try— *procrastinate, hyperbole, indignant.* Guess what they might mean by putting them in a sentence.

SPEAK UP FOR SUCCESS

PLTS objectives: building confidence in others, taking responsibility.

Skills objectives: speaking clearly and with confidence.

GET EXCITED!

Being able to speak with confidence is one of the most important skills you will ever need. Get used to the sound of your own voice by standing up straight, lifting your chin and projecting your voice to the back of the room saying the following slowly and clearly: 'Ladies and gentlemen. Welcome to the Communication Olympics where we are learning to become champion communicators.' Now try this tongue-twister to tune up your pronunciation: 'Peter Piper picked a pot of pickled peppers.'

MAIN ACTIVITY

Being a confident speaker is all in the mind. We can all speak but it is important to show enjoyment and enthusiasm when you are speaking. What makes a great speaker? Watch some examples of politicians and celebrities that impress you. Make a list of the qualities of a great speaker, e.g. smiling and standing up straight, keeping eye contact with the audience, speaking loudly and clearly.

Be a speech coach—your job is to make your partner feel great about speaking! In pairs take it in turns to talk for one minute about your favourite hobby, music or TV programme. Encourage your partner to speak loudly, clearly and confidently. Help your partner to practise visualising themselves as a famous speaker. Give them a couple of practice runs.

Score your coach! How confident did they make you feel about speaking? Mark the spot on the arrow.

Not confident   **Quite confident**   **Very confident**

Now work as a team with another pair coaching each other to become top children's TV presenters introducing their favourite television programme in a couple of sentences. When ready demonstrate your speaking to the class.

Use your Tracker Pack to rate yourself in your PLTS for this lesson.

BUILD YOUR OWN COUNTRY

Choose your tasks—or create your own!

5. Make a list of products that your country specialises in. Create a prototype of one. – 6 points

7. Create a website or leaflet to advertise holidays in your country – 5 points

8. Design a coat of arms or flag and slogan for your country – 2 points

9. Design a map of your country showing major landmarks, animal habitats and historic sites – 7 points

10. Write a day in the life of one of your citizens – 5 points

4. Write and deliver (record) a speech to celebrate your country – 5 points

3. Create a currency for our country. Work out the exchange rate and some examples of prices and salaries – 6 points

11. Explain the favourite sports of your country and what success they have achieved – 4 points

2. Compose and perform an anthem for your country – 6 points

1. Write the ten commandments for your country to demonstrate your culture, morals and religion – 4 points

14. Create your own task—check it out with your teacher – 10 points

13. Create a list of laws for your country – 3 points

12. Create a typical menu that represents traditional food from your country – 4 points

ECO-FESTIVAL

Choose your tasks—or create your own!

2. Compose the music for the introduction to the festival – 6 points

3. Research what a festival is and find out what makes them successful – 6 points

4. Write the timetable for the festival. Choose a variety of exciting activities for all ages – 4 points

5. Design a brochure to advertise your eco-festival – 5 points

6. Create a website for your festival with all the activities introduced – 4 points

7. List all the activities that should take place at a young people's eco-festival – 5 points

8. Create a menu for lunch at the eco-festival – 3 points

9. Research which products should be on display at the lunchtime exhibition during your festival – 3 points

10. Prepare a mime, play or dance that will demonstrate a theme from your festival – 6 points

1. Create a name and design a logo for your festival – 4 points

A, B, C. Create your own tasks—check it out with your teacher – 10 points

12. Design a mural that could be a legacy of the festival – 4 points

11. Write an opening speech for the festival and decide who will deliver it – 10 points

BAND AGE - CREATE A ROCK BAND FOR CHARITY

Choose your tasks—or create your own!

6. Create a website about your band. Include details of the charity they have chosen to raise money for – 4 points

5. Design costumes for your band's tour of the UK – 5 points

7. Write a letter to a famous international politician inviting them to your band's opening night – 5 points

8. Decide which charity your band will raise funds for and design a t-shirt to promote it – 3 points

9. Design a video storyboard for your band's first single – 3 points

4. Choose a name for your band. Write profiles of your band members – 4 points

3. Find out what genre of music would be popular for your band – 3 points

2. Write some lyrics for songs that highlight poverty and suffering in the world – 6 points

1. Design a CD cover for your band – 4 points

A, B, C. Create your own tasks—check it out with your teacher – 5 points

12. Record a radio interview with your band members – 4 points

11. Design the billboard advertisement for your band – 3 points

10. Plan an international tour for your band. Produce a brochure to advertise it – 6 points

GAMESHOW

Choose your tasks—or create your own!

6. Create a website for your gameshow to get the audience involved – 4 points

7. Write a letter from a would-be contestant saying why he/she wants to be on the show – 5 points

8. Choose three presenters that may be good for your show and list the pros and cons for each. Present to your group and let them decide the winner – 3 points

9. Write an email to your chosen presenter telling them about the show and inviting them to be the presenter – 3 points

5. Design a set for the gameshow – 5 points

4. Write the format and rules for the show—including the USP (unique selling point) – 4 points

3. Research three popular gameshows and find out what makes them successful – 6 points

2. Compose the music for the opening credits to the show and record it – 6 points

1. Create a name and design a logo for your gameshow – 4 points

A, B, C. Create your own tasks—check it out with your teacher – 5 points

12. Create a full page advertisement for your new show to be published in *TV Times* – 4 points

10. Create a storyboard showing how your gameshow will work – 6 points

11. Mock up a sample episode of your show to demonstrate it to the class – 10 points

FUTURE SCHOOL 2020

Choose your tasks—or create your own!

6. Create a website for your school. Include a page for students, parents and staff – 6 points

5. Design the school uniform for your school – 5 points

7. Write a letter to the Prime Minister inviting him to an event at your school – 5 points

8. Write an article for the local newspaper about the day your amazing new school opened – 3 points

9. Design a video storyboard for your school for new students – 3 points

4. Choose a name for your school and design the school badge – 4 points

10. Sketch a picture of your school as it looks from the front or a bird's-eye view – 6 points

3. Write a set of five rules for your future school – 3 points

2. Write a school song for your future school – 6 points

1. Design a new kind of desk and chair to fit in a classroom of the future – 5 points

A, B, C. Create your own tasks—check it out with your teacher – 5 points

12. Record a radio interview with students at your school – 4 points

11. Plan the timetable for your school for a typical Year 8 student – 4 points

PLTS Breakthrough Project:

....

Team: ....

Task number	Who?	Success criteria How will we know it's good?	PLTS developed	Subject links	Points awarded	Complete

A NEW LOOK AT HOMEWORK

EXTENDED LEARNING AT HOME TO DEVELOP THE PLTS

ACTIVITY 7
PLTS BREAKTHROUGH PROJECTS

STUDENT SHEET

We want to give you credit for all the learning you do at home! Earn points for doing the things that push you out of your comfort zone!

Ideas for extended learning that you do at home			
Home	**Hobbies/sports**	**Technology**	**Other**
Cooking/cleaning Gardening Fixing things Hosting friends Helping neighbours Washing/ironing Decorating Looking after pets Car washing/maintenance	Teams Crafts/art Guides/scouts Army Cadets Keep fit/gym Swimming Drama/dance Chess/games Music/singing/karaoke Walking/cycling Reading books/mags	Computer games Internet research Video/camera work Photography iPod — downloading etc. Communication networks Mobile phone Films	Charity work Holidays Boot sales/ garage sales

Examples	Commentary	PLTS developed	Points
Cooked an omelette	Never cooked before so got advice. Mix up eggs and milk, added salt and pepper. Melted butter in pan but it got a bit stuck.	Teamwork Effective participation Self-management	5 points
Army Cadets	Went as usual and learnt to march.	Teamwork Effective participation Self-management	3 points
Facebook	Found out how to write on my wall and download pictures.	Creative thinking Independent enquiry	3 points
Pets	Fed neighbour's cat as they are on holiday. It doesn't like water near its food! Gave it TLC too.	Self-management Independent enquiry	5 points

Points scored for effort and variety of out of school activity. The idea is to do lots of things at home and discuss how they help you learn. Your record sheet will be discussed with your tutor.

The Competency Curriculum Toolkit © Jackie Beere, Helen Boyle and Crown House Publishing Ltd

A NEW LOOK AT HOMEWORK - PAGE 2
EXTENDED LEARNING AT HOME TO DEVELOP THE PLTS

TARGET

Try to do as many different activities at home this term as you can and note what they are here. Assign the points you think you could earn from these activities. More points for more challenge! YOU decide …

Activity list	Points

Tracker Pack

Teacher's notes

The Tracker Pack is designed to motivate students to track their progress to becoming golden learners against the personal, learning and thinking skills (PLTS).

The first section of the Tracker Pack describes the PLTS—offering suggested guidance statements of how students might rate their PLTS progress and providing space for students to write targets for themselves.

Students should use the Tracker Pack at regular stages throughout competency project activities to provide opportunities for reflection on the progress they are making with their PLTS. They should be encouraged to have conversations with their peers, their teacher and themselves to review their PLTS progress. Students should mark and date a cross on the continuum arrow deciding whether they are performing at bronze, silver or gold level.

The statements in the Tracker Pack for bronze, silver and gold levels are suggested for guidance on how students might achieve these levels in the PLTS. These statements are only suggestions and teachers and students are encouraged to consider developing their own PLTS statements.

The three levels, bronze, silver and gold, can be replaced at the teacher's discretion with numbers (1, 2, 3), numbers (A, B, C), etc. to track progress if preferred. There is a progression summary sheet to record half-termly outcomes for reporting purposes.

At the bottom of each page in the Tracker Pack there is a space provided for praise, advice and targets.

Praise

The teacher, peers or the student can complete this section. It is for positive statements about successes they have achieved in their recent competency-based activities/project. It should contain an example of what they have done well (e.g. *I spoke clearly and with confidence to the whole class about my team's work and effort*).

Advice

The teacher or the students' peers should complete this section. It is a space for them to write about mistakes the student can learn from. It should contain an example from their recent competence-based activities/project (e.g. *When you act as a team leader you need to make sure everyone in your team contributes*).

Targets

The student should complete this section in consultation with the teacher about a target they can set themselves to enable them to gain a better medal position in future PLTS learning (e.g. *I want to achieve a silver medal next time for personal skills/team workers. I will take the challenge of being a team leader again and not just work with my close friends. I will make sure everyone takes a turn in sharing their views*).

TRACKER PACK - PAGE 1

USING THE PLTS TO BECOME A GOLDEN LEARNER

What are we looking for? For each of the competences you can mark a cross where you think you have performed for this project or lesson (you can add the date too and your initials).

Personal skills (P)		
Team workers *Young people work confidently with others, adapting to different contexts and taking responsibility for their own part. They listen and value different views, resolving issues and creating sustainable relationships.*	**Team workers** I can work in a team to achieve common goals. I can compromise with others in my group. I can adapt to play many different roles in a group. I can show kindness to team players. I can take responsibility and I am confident in my contribution. I can give feedback to other team members and groups.	Write your P targets here:
Effective participators *Young people who actively engage with issues that affect them and those around them. They play a full part in their school, college, workplace or community and take responsible action to improve life for everyone.*	**Effective participators** I can willingly take part and change issues that affect our lives. I can make a persuasive case for action. I can listen to other viewpoints and work as a negotiator to reach workable solutions. I know that people have different ethics and these should be respected. I understand that being a good citizen involves helping the community.	
Learning (L)		
Self-managers *Young people who organise themselves, showing personal responsibility, initiative, creativity and enterprise with a commitment to learning and self-improvement.*	**Reflective Learners** I can assess others and myself and can give positive feedback. I can set my own goals and targets. I can analyse my work and improve it. I can accept positive and negative feedback. I can improve on my mistakes for future progress. I can confidently present my work in front of an audience.	Write your L targets here:

TRACKER PACK - PAGE 2

USING THE PLTS TO BECOME A GOLDEN LEARNER

Learning (L) cntd		Write your L targets here:
Reflective learners	**Self-managers**	
Young people can evaluate their strengths and limitations and set themselves realistic goals with criteria for success. They monitor their own performance and progress, inviting feedback and adapting their learning effectively.	I seek out challenges and new responsibilities. I react well to changing the plan that I have made. I keep going when the going gets tough. I can deal with pressure and deadlines then seek help when I need it. I can set myself targets and work towards them. I show initiative and take risks.	
Thinking (T)		Write your T targets here:
Independent enquirers	**Independent learners**	
Young people who can process and evaluate information in their investigations, planning what to do and how to go about it. They recognise others have different beliefs and attitudes.	I can plan and do research, taking into consideration the consequences of my decision. I can think deeply about a subject, putting myself in other people's shoes. I can look at and write about information, deciding how important it is. I can take into consideration different beliefs and feelings when making decisions. I back up my ideas with thought about arguments and evidence.	

TRACKER PACK - PAGE 3

USING THE PLTS TO BECOME A GOLDEN LEARNER

Thinking (T) *cntd*		Write your L targets here:
Creative thinkers *Young people think creatively by generating and exploring ideas and making original connections. They try different ways to tackle a problem, working with others to find imaginative solutions.*	**Creative thinkers** I can come up with ideas and explore other possibilities. I can ask questions about a topic to make me think in more depth. I can combine mine and other people's ideas and past experiences to compromise, where needed, and think of new ideas as a result. I can question whether assumptions we make are accurate. I try out new ways of solving problems and pursue ideas. I can change/compromise ideas to fit new circumstances.	

PERSONAL SKILLS – HOW DID I DO?

For each of the competences you can mark a cross where you think you have performed for this project or activity (you can add the date too and your initials).

PLTS assessment			

PLTS – typical traits	Bronze	Silver	Gold
Personal skills • Team workers • Effective participators	'I find it hard to get on with others' 'I only want to work with my friends' 'I don't really care about other people in the world' 'I lose my temper easily'	'I like working in groups' 'I listen to other people's opinions' 'I care about the rest of the world' 'I want to do the right thing' 'I take part in a club at school' 'I want to work hard and do well in the future' 'I am interested in the news'	'My aim is that our group does well on the project' 'I think a lot about how I can help solve issues in the world' 'I have volunteered to help out in my community' 'I have a variety of hobbies and interests' 'I am always thinking of ideas and projects' 'I know just what I want to be in the future—even if it changes each week!' 'People get on with me and I know how to get on with all sorts of different people' 'I believe I can do anything I set my mind on and most of all I want to help other people'

Praise:..

Advice: ....

Targets: ....

LEARNING SKILLS - HOW DID I DO?

For each of the competences you can mark a cross where you think you have performed for this project or activity. You can add the date too and your initials.

Me:

Teacher:

PLTS – typical traits	Bronze	Silver	Gold
Learning skills • Self-managers • Reflective learners	'I am a kinaesthetic learner so get bored listening' 'I only work when I am interested' 'I rarely finish my work' 'I can't see the point in learning'	'I am learning to use my brain in various ways' 'Making mistakes is an important part of learning' 'I make lists of things I have to do' 'I think carefully when I work out how to improve my work' 'I know learning means hard work and lots of practice'	'I believe I can learn to be more clever if I work hard enough' 'I really learn from making mistakes' 'I like a challenge as it makes me learn more' 'I always have a plan' 'I believe I can do anything if I try hard enough' 'I am growing my brain through extending my learning styles' 'I like getting feedback about how I am doing so that I can improve' 'If something doesn't work then I try a different way, then a different way until it works' 'I am able to draft and re-draft my work until it is right'

Praise: ....

Advice: ....

Targets: ....

THINKING SKILLS - HOW DID I DO?

For each of the competences you can mark a cross where you think you have performed for this project or activity (you can add the date too and your initials).

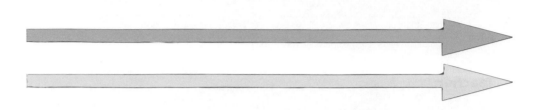

PLTS – typical traits	Bronze	Silver	Gold
Thinking skills • Independent enquirers • Creative thinkers	'I don't like thinking too much' 'I prefer to be told what to do' 'I can't think of ideas easily' 'I can't do it' 'I can't see how to do it' 'I can't be bothered' 'I don't like to be different'	'I like to work on my own sometimes' 'I can think of ideas and get others to help me' 'I will ask questions to help me with my work' 'I enjoy new situations and meeting new people' 'I can work well on my own'	'I always have lots of ideas' 'I like to work out why as well as how' 'I get on with my work and often do things that the teacher didn't ask for' 'I get very involved in my projects and usually go off in new directions' 'I like asking difficult questions' 'There is no limit to how much I can learn' 'I have my own individual style' 'I like to try many different solutions until I get it right' 'I like to know how things work for myself'

Praise:...

Advice: ....

Targets: ....

PLTS PROGRESSION SUMMARY SHEET (SAMPLE)

	Activity 1	Activity 2	Activity 3	Activity 4	Activity 5	Activity 6	End of year summary
Personal skills (P)	Bronze	Silver	Silver	Gold	Silver	Gold	**Silver+**
Learning skills (L)	Silver	Bronze	Gold	Gold	Silver	Gold	**Gold-**
Thinking skills (T)	Bronze	Bronze	Bronze	Silver	Silver	Silver	**Bronze+**
PLTS summary	**Bronze+**	**Bronze+**	**Silver**	**Gold-**	**Silver**	**Gold-**	**Silver**

Note: Numbers or letters can be substituted if statistical data is required.

Glossary

APP	Assessment of Pupil Progress. It is intended that these progression models from QCA will show how students demonstrate the level they have achieved in subjects, in order to provide summative assessment
Assessment for learning	Assessment that contributes to the learning process, usually identified with research by Black and Wiliam
Cognitive skills	Another name for thinking skills
Competency/competence skills	Clusters of skills, abilities, expertise—usually more practical ability
Competency-based curriculum	A curriculum that delivers personal, learning and thinking skills as well as knowledge/content in a cross-curricular model
Emotional intelligence	The ability to manage thinking and emotions in order to be effective
Empathy	The ability to understand another's viewpoint
Experiential learning	Learning by practical experience
Formative assessment	Assessment that forms part of the learning process and relates to assessment for learning
Learning styles	Individual methods and modes of learning
Learning to Learn	The term used for programmes of study that teach students about neuroscience and learning styles in order to support their learning skills (see the Campaign for Learning research project directed by Newcastle University)
Metacognition	Reflecting on thinking and learning
Multiple intelligence	A model of intelligence first cited by Howard Gardner that demonstrates cognitive ability as displayed in a variety of ways beyond literacy and numeracy
Opening Minds	The Royal Society of Arts (RSA) model for cross-curricular teaching to develop student competences
Peer-assessment	Judging the performance of a peer against criteria
PLTS	The Personal, Learning and Thinking Skills defined by QCA
SEAL	Social and Emotional Aspects of Learning—a set of resources and guidance provided to improve well-being and performance in schools (see http://www.bandapilot.org for a range of resources)

Self-assessment	Judging one's own performance against criteria
Summative assessment	Assessment at the end of a course that demonstrates learning
Tracker Pack	A pack of materials on the accompanying CD that provide opportunities for self-assessment and peer-assessment of the PLTS
Transferrable skills	Abilities and skills that can be transferred from one context to another

Bibliography

Amabile, T. M., *Growing Up Creative* (New York: Crown Publishing, 1989).

Beare, H., *Creating the Future School* (London: Routledge/Falmer, 2001).

Beere, J., *The Key Stage 3 Learning Kit* (Sussex: Connect Publications, 2002).

Beere, J., *The Learner's Toolkit* (Camarthen: Crown House, 2007).

Bloom, B. et al, *Brain, Mind and Behaviour* (New York: W.H. Freeman and Co, 1988).

Bosher, M., and Hazlewood, P., *Nurturing Independent Thinkers* (Stafford: Network Educational Press, 2006).

Bransford, J. D., Brown, A. L. and Cocking, R. R. (eds.), *How People Learn: Brain, Mind, Experience and School* (Washington, DC: CBASSE, 2000).

Claxton, G., *Hare Brain, Tortoise Mind* (London: Fourth Estate, 1997).

Demos, *About Learning: Report of the Learning Group* (London: Demos, 2005).

Friedman, T. L.. *The World is Flat* (London: Penguin, 2005).

Gardner, H., *Frames of Mind: The Theory of Multiple Intelligence* (London: Montana, 1984).

Gatto, J. T., *Dumbing Us Down: The Hidden Curriculum of Compulsory Schooling* (Philadelphia, PA: New Society Publishers, 2006).

Gilbert, C., *2020 Vision: The Report of the Teaching and Learning in 2020 Review Group* (London: DfES, 2007).

Goleman, D., *Emotional Intelligence: Why It Can Matter More Than IQ* (London: Bloomsbury, 1996).

Hazlewood, P., *Marlborough School: Nurturing Independent Thinkers*. RSA Opening Minds Project (Stafford: Network Educational Press, 2005).

Jensen, E., *The Learning Brain* (Huntsville, AL: Turning Point, 1995).

John, A., *Punished by Rewards: The Trouble with Gold Stars, Incentive Plans, A's, Praise, and Other Bribes* (Boston, MA: Houghton Mifflin, 1999).

Middlewood, D., Parker, R. and Beere, J., *Creating a Learning School* (London: Paul Chapman, 2005).

MacClean, P., *The Triune Brain in Evolution* (New York: Plenum, 1990).

Piaget, J., *Play, Dreams and Imitation in Childhood* (London: Heineman, 1945).

Royal Society of Arts, *Opening Minds: Giving Young People a Better Chance* (London: RSA, 2005).

Toffler, A., and Gibson, R. (eds), *Rethinking the Future* (London: Nicholas Brearley Publishing, 1996).

West-Burnham, J. *The School of the Future* (location: Headlines, 2000).

Wiliam, D. and Black, P., *Inside the Black Box* (London: NFER Nelson, 2006).

Websites

http://www.qca.org.uk
http://www.thersa.org
http://www.openingminds.org.uk
http://www.sage.pub.co.uk
http://www.jackiebeere.com

Curriculum links

http://curriculum.qca.org.uk/key-stages-3-and-4/index.aspx
http://curriculum.qca.org.uk/key-stages-3-and-4/cross-curriculum-dimensions/globaldimension/index.aspx

Index